Fierce Love

A Bold Path to
Ferocious Courage
and Rule-Breaking
Kindness That Can
Heal the World

Fierce Love

Rev. Dr. Jacqui Lewis

R A N D O M   H O U S E
L A R G E   P R I N T

Published in the United States of America by Random House Large Print in association with Harmony Books, an imprint of Random House, a division of Penguin Random House LLC, New York.

Cover design by Sandra Chiu

The Library of Congress has established a Cataloging-in-Publication record for this title.

ISBN: 978-0-593-50851-0

www.penguinrandomhouse.com/large-print-format-books

FIRST LARGE PRINT EDITION

Printed in the United States of America

1st Printing

This Large Print edition published in accord with the standards of the N.A.V.H.

For Mom and Dad—my first fierce loves

Contents

You, Yours, and Ours

Even before COVID-19 showed up in our global family, we were living in what I call "hot-mess times." In our current context, race and ethnicity, caste and color, gender and sexuality, socioeconomic status and education, religion and political party have all become reasons to divide and be conquered by fear and rancor. For some time a perfect storm has been brewing, one that polarizes, amplifying the power of divergent ideologies and reducing our differences to shallow and bigoted categories in which "we" are vehemently against "them." Put simply, we are in a perilous time, and the answer to the question "Who are we to be?" will have implications for generations to come.

We have a choice to make. We can answer this question with diminished imagination, by closing ranks with our tribe and hiding from our human responsibility to heal the world. Or we can answer the question of who we are to be another way: We can answer it in the spirit of **ubuntu**. The concept comes from the Zulu phrase **Umuntu ngumuntu ngabantu**, which literally means that a person is a person through other people. Another translation is, "I am who I am because we are who we are." When Zulus see each other, they offer this greeting: **Sawubona**, which means "I see you." And the response is **Sikhona**, which means "I exist." With this in mind, **who I will be** is deeply related to **who you are**. In other words, we are each impacted by the circumstances that impact those around us. What hurts you hurts me. What heals you heals me. What causes you joy causes me to rejoice, and what makes you sad also causes me to weep.

By channeling the ancient wisdom of ubuntu, we can engineer a badly needed love revolution to rise up out of the ashes of our current reality. I'm not referring to the sentimental love of romantic comedies, greeting cards, and pop music—**that** kind of love does not serve this purpose. No, I'm calling for a demanding, heart-transforming, **fierce** love. Fierce love breaks through tribalism to help humans realize an inextricable and irrevocable connection, and understand that the liberation, livelihood, and thriving of people and planet are tied up together. In this moment, in the urgency of now, we simply **must** ask questions of identity as we consider the surviving and thriving of all peoples. We must allow the stories of others—the vulnerable, the poor, the stranger, the one least like us—to change our stories, to impact our story. The empathy that grows from listening to others, from connecting with our neighbors, and from loving our neighbors as we love ourselves can define the courses of action we take. How we vote, where we live, where we shop, how we raise our children, how we care for the planet: All of these choices, when made with ubuntu, can save humanity.

I love a good story. Stories can horrify you, make you cry, shock you, and shake you to your core. They can melt your heart, change your mind, call you to action. Humans become human because of stories. They form our identity, remind us of who we've been, and teach us who we are to be. We lean into them, fall back from them; we wrestle with their contradictions, we sort them out.

This book is packed with stories: stories of sacrifice and resilience, stories of truth-telling and forgiveness. Most of these stories come from deep in my own history—from both my childhood and my adult life—though there are others here, too, as testimony to what fierce love can do. My stories are of my own awakening—psychological, sexual, political, and spiritual—and trace my journey to confront and make amends with myself, my family, my community, and my God. Coincidentally, fire is a recurring character in the forging of my identity and outlook. When I was in my twenties, a moving-truck fire took almost all of my earthly belongings, and in 2020—just as I was finishing this manuscript—a suspicious fire that started next door to my church in Manhattan consumed all but the façade of my beloved workplace. I realize that both fires gave back to me as much as they took. I learned the liberation that comes when you lose everything, that the opportunity to begin again is true freedom. Especially after the Middle Church fire, I've been revisited with the tremendous power of ubuntu in the way that people all over the world have grieved with our congregation, loved on us fiercely, and pledged to help us rebuild. **What hurts you hurts me, what heals you heals me**, writ large.

Whether my own or plucked from the world, the stories I share illustrate my thinking about how to live with ubuntu and to effect change. There are nine of these strategies, nine behaviors that fall into three categories: those that relate to you and the way you think about and treat yourself; those about how you behave in your community; and those about how you choose to amplify your personal code out in the world. I've made these tenets concrete in my life, and you can make them concrete in yours. These practices are tools to help you become kinder and gentler; to build quality relationships and communities that are inclusive and intersectional; to create a culture that embraces the full spectrum of ethnicity, gender, sexuality, and humanity that make this world, and this life, so amazing. All of us must face and embrace the urgent need for deep social change—change that begins within, then spreads like ripples on a pond, and finally becomes a tsunami of love-inspired change. No matter your age, race, faith, gender, or sexuality, I hope these nine practices give you a new sense of the power you have to be good and to insist on good; to care for others and insist on being cared for; to stand up for the vulnerable and stand against injustice; to love and be loved.

As a scholar who has studied religion and psychology, as an author of books on identity development and the power of stories, as a professor who teaches about leadership and anti-racist work, I understand why and how people and systems change. I know this to be true: The world doesn't get great unless we **all** get better. If there is such a thing as salvation, then we are not saved until everyone is saved; our dignity and liberation are bound together. We must care for ourselves and the village around us. If we don't, the village's problems become our problems, and together our children will continue to hide from bullets in their classrooms. Our elders' safety nets will be threatened. Our young adults will face mounting debt and earn less than their parents. Fear, xenophobia, racism, bigotry—these problems belong to all of us, and they will get better as we all get better! When it comes to truly thriving, those of us who are "woke" and those of us who are awakening know that the glow of our fabulous, wonderful lives dims when our communities are suffering and unable to stretch toward a future just as fabulous as the future we want for our loved ones and ourselves.

By telling stories of my own struggle to care for **me, mine, and ours**; by sharing the experiences of good people who have shifted their lives and the society around them; by sharing wisdom and insights from many disciplines; and by providing guideposts for the journey toward ubuntu ethics and fierce love, I hope this book will illuminate a beautiful future awaiting all of us. I can see a bold new path led by a vision of the sacred goodness of humankind and the abundance of the planet's resources. I can see it, and I want you to see it, too. You and I are the ones we've been waiting for to create better lives for ourselves and our communities and to build a better world—together. All we need is the courage to imagine, and the will to make it be so.

Fierce
Love

YOU

Perhaps we should love ourselves so fiercely, that when others see us, they know exactly how it should be done.

—Rudy Francisco

Chapter One

Love Yourself Unconditionally. It All Starts Here.

Love yourself first and everything else falls into line.
—Lucille Ball

Loving yourself unconditionally is a tall order, but as a daily practice it's essential. Self-love is like fuel in the tank of our souls. I hate to admit it, but when my reservoir of self-love is hovering on empty, I'm cranky, short-tempered, and quicker to anger. When I'm feeling low about myself, I'm not a loving presence to my husband, family, and friends; I don't listen as well, and I can be defensive. In my professional life, when the self-love meter is low, I overfunction and my workaholism resurfaces.

I fall in and out of love with myself every year,

sometimes on the same day. I'll preach a sermon that really lands, then open my e-mail that evening and see I've received yet another hateful message from a stranger; apparently, a woman in a leadership position still rankles some. Or I'll be standing at the grill, enjoying the smell of smoke on the breeze, and decide to call my eighty-five-year-old dad because barbecuing is our shared passion. I tell him some personal things, some celebratory things, and he says something he thinks is funny but is actually awkward, and a little painful. Old wounds flood my heart, and I'm back in my eighteen-year-old story, feeling sorrow and uncertainty. I might be at a Black Lives Matter rally, full of purpose and power. But then I turn on the news when I get home and see the story of one more dead Black person, and I'm pulled low. To be honest, it's so hard to love myself when the culture pushes the message that Black bodies like mine are dangerous, unworthy, and expendable. Some days I want to curl up and watch **Black Panther** over and over again; I'd rather be in the beautiful world of Wakanda, I think, than in the United States, where I live.

Let's face it: This nation is an environment in which it is difficult for **any of us** to learn to love ourselves well. Our history—our shared story—is one fraught with violence and oppression. British colonizers left their homes and sailed the seas, seeking freedom for themselves but gaining it by taking land (and life) from those who already inhabited the land they called Turtle Island. The economy of this brave new world was built on the labor of indentured servants and enslaved Africans. Our founding fathers wrote lofty ideals into documents that did not confer inalienable rights on the poor, the Indigenous, the African, or women. Over time, all of us who are not Anglo-Saxon, Protestant, wealthy, straight men have been denied full access to the American dream.

These national narratives—white is right; grab power by any means necessary; God is Christian; queer is wrong; women are the weaker sex; keep what you steal; lies are true until discovered—have wormed their way inside of all our stories. These negative concepts impact our ability to love ourselves and therefore one another. To create a more loving and just society, we have to dig deep into our stories, sift through the good, the bad, and the ugly, and find the meaningful moments that source self-love.

Just as the story of our nation shapes us, all the stories in our lives make us who we are. Stories carry the details of the relationships and experiences that form us. Birth order, gender, religion, sexuality, racial identity—these are just some of the stories that are woven together to make a self. They tell us something about the contexts in which we've become who we are, the environments in which we have grown. They tell us how our parents responded when we were hungry or afraid, how our teachers reacted to our abilities in the classroom, what our lovers communicated to us when we were dating.

To foster more love for ourselves, we need to look deeply at these stories and search them for meaning, for lessons. When we do this, we'll learn about our childhood, about how our loved ones held us, showed up for us. Were they more absent than present? Who filled in the gaps for us, to help us know we were shiny and wonderful? Examining our stories, we'll learn about our own behavior with the people we love. Did we show up for them? Were we angry, bitter, gentle, kind?

It takes courage to peer into our stories and see what's there; it's like looking into a mirror. It can be eye-opening, and we can be startled by what we see. Writing this book—opening up my story to you and for myself—has required Advil, frequent breaks, and a nightly glass of red wine! I think it's worth it, though, as part of my ongoing work, to look closely at my story and see what's really happening inside. Toward the goal of finding self-love and self-compassion, you also need to do this work, to take a good look at yourself and the world around you, to see what's what. How did you get to be you? Can you love **you** better? When we look in the story-mirror, we'll see cringe-worthy moments that challenge our best view of ourselves, moments we wish we could cancel or delete. But we'll also revisit the times we overcame those regrettable experiences and affirm the best of ourselves and our capacity for love of self and others. It takes grace to keep it all in front of us—the embarrassing moments and the moments of great joy and affirmation. Accepting ourselves, forgiving ourselves—this is what unconditional love is about.

———

It takes grace to keep it all in front of us—the embarrassing moments and the moments of great joy and affirmation. Accepting ourselves, forgiving ourselves— this is what unconditional love is about.

———

What I Learned in Kindergarten

When I look deep into my stories, I find myself back in kindergarten. It was 1964, and our family lived on Pease Air Force Base, in Portsmouth, New Hampshire. Being at school on the base meant being with Mrs. Easley—a joyful woman, with a gently wrinkled face, white hair, and deep-blue eyes that twinkled like stars. And it meant sitting in a circle singing, learning, and laughing with friends. Tired from mornings of spelling and building with blocks, we ate lunch and then took naps on cots under our desks.

Occasionally, for a special afternoon treat, we churned butter together, turning sweet milk into a salty spread for Ritz crackers, each bite savored just before we went home. It felt like taking a delicious mouthful of Mrs. Easley's love home with me.

I usually walked home with my two best friends, both named Tommy. Tommy Holly was a gorgeous blond boy with eyes the color of the sky. He had lost and found his two front teeth, so they loomed large in his smile. Tommy Hollister was Dennis the Menace in the flesh, with red hair, freckles, a temper, and a penchant for striped shirts. He was a cartoon come to life. Chivalrous before knowing what that meant, the Tommys took turns putting my chair up on the table at the end of each day, so the janitor could mop, and setting it down on the floor again the next morning. The three of us always sat close together, even during lunch and snacktime; we were inseparable.

Freshly churned butter was a wonderful taste from kindergarten days, but I also had my first bitter taste of hate in the spring, when a girl named Lisa moved to our base from Mississippi. She was a pretty little girl, with dark brown eyes and blond hair cut short. One day, she squeezed between me and Tommy Holly and stage-whispered: "You're not supposed to be friends with her, you know. She's a nasty nigger. And she gets chocolate milk from her mama's tits."

A **nigger**. I don't think I'd ever heard this word before. Mom and Dad never said it. In fact, even after my siblings and I were old enough to spell, if we were within earshot when they described people, our parents spelled w-h-i-t-e, A-s-i-a-n,

S-p-a-n-i-s-h, and N-e-g-r-o. When I asked them about this later, my folks explained they were trying to shelter us from the consciousness of race and racism in our nation.

Though I didn't know the word, when Lisa spat out what I came to understand as the N-word, I knew she was being unkind. Her nastiness made me feel nasty. I have no idea how I knew to say this or where I had heard it, but I put my hands on my hips and said: "White cracker, white cracker, you don't shine. I bet you five dollars I can beat your behind." It was as though Lisa and I were in a grown-up play, interacting in ways and with words that someone else scripted.

At that age, I vaguely understood that there were tensions in the American South. I had sipped cool water from a Colored fountain outside the courthouse in Ruleville, Mississippi, when visiting my grandmother. I had heard the story of Emmett Till, a Black boy killed for whistling at a white woman, a fact that was later called into question. I knew that when Mom and Dad were little, they had to walk a long way from their homes, past the "regular" schools to the ones for Colored people. But those stories were from down South, far away. And now Lisa had brought Mississippi with her to my happy little classroom. Right there, in my safe space in New Hampshire, she turned the N-word on me like a Southern police officer turning a fire hose on protesters.

At the dinner table, I told my parents about Lisa—her name calling, my hurt feelings, and my defensive response. I told them that Lisa would soon have a birthday party, and that I was pretty sure I would not be invited.

Mom called me to her and, holding my face in her hands, said:

"Jac, believe it or not, some people will not like you because you are a Negro. Isn't that silly? But remember, God loves you very much, and so do we. You are our child; you are special, you can do and be anything you want if you work hard. And don't call people names, Jac. We don't do that."

Along with dinner, Mom nourished me that evening with a way to think about and deal with bigotry. By dismissing Lisa's taunt as **silly**, she took the sting out of it and even made me feel a little sorry for Lisa's ignorance. That night, when Mom and I knelt by my bed to pray, along with "Now I lay me down to sleep," I added a child's wish: "Please, God, make it be so that no matter what color people are, they will be loved." I remember that I wanted everyone—the people who looked like me, the people who looked like Lisa, and all the folks of every shade—to feel special and loved.

My father's response, however, taught me that though Lisa's language and beliefs may have been silly, they were not without consequence. The next morning, Dad went to the air force base commander and reported the incident. He demanded that Lisa be made to apologize to me, and that her father apologize to him. The commander agreed and called Lisa's father to his office, where he immediately apologized. The following Monday, Lisa apologized to me and invited me to her party. She performed this farce in front of the two Tommys, in the circle during snacktime. Even at that young age, it seemed to me that her apology had the same mean spirit as her earlier taunt.

That Saturday, I joined a bunch of my classmates at Lisa's house. We played, ate cake, and watched as she opened her presents. I had as good a time as a child can when they are invited to a party under those circumstances. The party wasn't great, and the apology was hollow, but I felt that my parents and I had won something together.

Picking up this story and looking at it closely, I'd say Lisa **raced** me. Before our encounter, I was Jacqueline Janette Lewis, **Jac**—Emma's baby, Richard's child—a little girl named for the elegant and brilliant wife of a presidential candidate. I was young, gifted, Black—a Negro in those days. But with the words she chose, Lisa baptized me into the racism of our nation.

I wonder now how my folks knew how to handle that moment in just the right way. They must have been so traumatized. The foul stench of racism had wafted all the way from Mississippi to New Hampshire, seeping through the barriers they had erected to protect themselves and their family. Mom didn't give me a history lesson about the Jim and Jane Crow-ness of her childhood; those lessons would come later. Instead, she helped me see that the notion that white folks were better than Black folks was **silly**, and that love was stronger than hate. Dad didn't roar and rage at the violation I suffered; he showed me how to be an activist. Before Black Lives Matter was a hashtag or a movement, and even as the Southern Freedom Movement was working for voting rights and equality, my dad was demanding respect and reparations.

I think my folks were tuned in to me as a precocious little person. They used this moment to **story** for me: You are loved, and you can handle racism with courageous truth-telling and moral courage. In that moment, they storied and mirrored for me what the late congressman John Lewis often said: "When you see something that is not right, not fair, not just, you have to speak up. You have to say something; you have to do something." Reflecting on this story puts more self-love in my tank, helping me to fight for justice yet another day.

Learning How to Love Yourself

To be good to others, you must practice being good to yourself. And no matter who we are or where we come from, no matter who we love and how we earn a living, the admonition to love your neighbor as you love yourself, when lived out, expresses the interdependence humans need in order to survive and thrive. And the first step, the starting place, is self-love. In the Greek language, the phrases "love neighbor" and "love yourself" are connected by the word **os**, which is like an equal sign. This suggests we are called to love the self **and** the neighbor in exactly the same way. When we don't love ourselves, it is impossible to love our neighbor.

Self-love goes in our tank when we are seen, known, and loved. All along our life cycle, even before we have language, we are seen into existence. When my grandson Octavius was beginning to crawl, I loved watching him watch his mother, Gabby. He was discovering what his hands could do, learning to scoot across the floor, and finding joy in his feet. This baby loved to bite his toes. When he did, he'd look up at Gabby, my daughter-in-law, who was smiling, laughing, delighting in him. Seeing her delight, he laughed hard in a surprisingly deep voice. Octavius looked away, tried something else, scooted his way toward his mom, and turned his attention fully to her. Once again, he'd see Mommy seeing him. Gabby was holding up a mirror for him that said: "I see you, little man. I see you learning, trying, biting your toes. I see you scooting around, holding up your head. You are funny, you are curious, and I love you!" What was being **seen** by his mom and his dad, Joel, began to exist for Octavius in a real way, shaping who he was becoming. He is older now, and he knows he's funny; he knows his parents and grandparents delight in his laughter. Octavius also knows how to demand what he wants by crying, and rewards us with laughter when he gets it. In other words, he is seeing us into existence as well!

We all need mirroring, no matter our age. When I watch Gabby being a phenomenal mom and I celebrate her mothering with praise, I hold up a mirror, I show her the image of her capability. This image sustains her when Octavius and big sister Ophelia are tired and crying, and sapping Gabby of her patience or energy. When we celebrate our employees with "Great job, thank you!" we add to the story of their work/career, and mirror their giftedness, which might sustain their drive and ambition to rise up the corporate ladder. When we go to the theater and stand to applaud the performers, we let them know we see their creativity. When we've cooked for our family and they have seconds and make the sounds that delicious food deserves, they hold up a mirror in which we see ourselves as nurturing. When my husband, John, reads these pages and says, "I get this," he sees me as "author," which helps put yet more self-love in my tank.

During the COVID-19 pandemic that plagued our globe and forced us to socially distance, many of us lost our mirrors; we lost the in-person connections that saw us, affirmed us, hugged us, and held us close. Two of my young friends—Sam and Isaac—speak to me often of how rough it is to be thirtysomething, single, and living on Zoom. Though they have not had COVID-19, they've suffered from the ways the disease isolated them from their communities. Sam once said: "Too many of us are out here lonely, hating our lives, and pretending we are okay. But we're not." These men missed the mirroring that occurs in community, which depleted their self-love tank. I get it. I **love** to preach, and preaching live from my home office grew difficult. I missed my congregation so much—the call-and-response, the eye contact, and the hugs after worship that mirrored, "We see you, Jacqui, and we love you."

The connection between self-love and the love of others is as old as time. From the moment we stood up and walked out of lonely caves and into the light of tribal togetherness, humans understood the inextricable connection, that our lives are woven together in love. Almost all the world's great religions encourage us to love our neighbor as ourselves. Sometimes called the Golden Rule, this beautiful teaching invites humans to treat one another—and in some traditions **all** creatures—the way we want to be treated. We're encouraged to choose for our neighbor what we want for ourselves, to celebrate their success as our own. Some traditions extend this neighbor-love to strangers as well. One tradition simply encourages followers to not hurt anyone's heart. The story embedded in these teachings across faiths and religions is: We belong to a mutually beneficial web of connection, well-being, and love. At the root of this connection is empathy; the result is kindness, compassion, respect, and understanding. When religion doesn't center on this mutuality, it can become one of the toxic narratives that, in the end, dismantles self-love.

The world's religions and the ubuntu philosophy remind me that each of us is who we are because of what the collective is. Thriving is a shared objective, achieved when we love our neighbor—even the stranger—the way we love ourselves. This means that when our neighbor is hungry, our stomachs growl and we aim to feed everyone.

———

The world's religions and the
ubuntu philosophy remind me that
each of us is who we are because
of what the collective is. Thriving is
a shared objective, achieved when
we love our neighbor—even
the stranger—the way
we love ourselves. This means that
when our neighbor is hungry, our
stomachs growl and we
aim to feed everyone.

———

I learned more about this connection among humans while visiting Robben Island, the South African prison where Nelson Mandela was confined in a tiny cell for eighteen of the twenty-seven years he was behind bars. I found it miraculous that Mandela could see his inextricable connection to the humanity of his captors, the ones who took away his liberty and humiliated him daily. He observed that no one is born hating another because of race, religion, or background. Mandela understood that just as hate is taught, love must be taught.

For some folks, talk about love sounds weak, but from my point of view love is the strongest force on the planet. I learned my favorite definition of **love** from one of my seminary professors, the late Dr. James E. Loder. He defined **love** as a "non-possessive delight in the particularity of the other." All these years later, I am still so moved by this sentiment. **Non-possessive delight** sounds like devotion to me. Rather than trying to change, manipulate, or devour the object of our affection, fierce love delights in the particularities of who they are. So, when you love yourself, you take delight in the unique particularities that add up to **you**, without judgment.

We've all seen what it looks like when someone has low self-love. I had a high school teacher who basically hazed us through a semester. She told our class that it had been difficult for her to get through her senior year and graduate, that it had been like walking on hot rocks, that **her** teacher had discouraged her at every turn. She had suffered a lifetime of disapproval; there weren't many mirrors reflecting that she was good, smart, and worthy of success. It seemed to me that she was repeating a pattern, which can happen if we don't examine our stories well and learn what they have to teach us. She was putting our class through the same difficult process she endured.

When I take a breath and reflect on that woman, I can almost see her younger self, her feeling-unloved self, and I have compassion for that girl. She felt passed over, dismissed, unseen. How many more people are bumping around on the subway or crossing busy streets without true self-love? How many folks, low on self-love, take to social media to post and say horrible things? Are they making decisions about budgets and policies, policing cities and towns, while running empty on self-love? Are they mean, selfish, or violent because there is a hole in their souls where more love could be? Maybe the racists and misogynists don't love themselves enough. The ones trying to build walls against immigrants or keep them in cages; the ones with their knees on the necks of Black people; the ones who withhold justice from gay people—what if their core issue is that they never learned to love themselves? What if this is true about the ones working to make the poor even poorer, who don't believe there are enough resources for all of us? What if they don't love themselves enough, or at all?

The same kind of gentle, receptive self-love that I'm encouraging is the soft spot in which love for others will grow. The way you love yourself is the first and crucial step in this program of nine practices in the discipline of fierce love. Toward that end, I ask you to reflect on the connection between your story and the story of the other. What do your stories have in common? Do you need to forgive yourself so you can forgive them? Loving yourself will help you to be curious about others, compassionate toward others, as gracious to your neighbor as you are to yourself.

I want to be clear: By self-love, I don't mean selfishness, self-absorption, or conceit. We all know people who hog the stage, dominate conversations, and have to be the center of attention, and I'm not arguing for that behavior. I'm also not arguing for narcissism, an exaggerated sense of self-importance that requires constant admiration. No, by self-love I mean a healthy delight in your true, imperfect, uniquely wonderful, particular self. I mean an unconditional appreciation for who you are, head to toe, inside and out: quirks, foibles, beauty, and blemishes—all of it. I mean seeing yourself truthfully and loving what you see.

Loving yourself will help you
to be curious about others,
compassionate toward others, as
gracious to your neighbor as you
are to yourself.

Honestly, the stories playing out in the world can make it difficult to love yourself, and therefore your neighbor. Messages from the culture that you don't matter, not just because of your race, but because of your gender, sexuality, economic status, or religion, can thwart self-love. Though her skin gives her some privilege, a white child might grow up in a context of poverty or domestic violence that can cripple her self-love. A child traveling across deserts and rivers to emigrate with his parents might lose some of his self-love in the wilderness. Even if you're born into circumstances that others consider ideal, messages in the culture can signal that you're not good enough, light enough, thin enough, smart enough, feminine or masculine enough to measure up to some ideal. The space between those ideals and your realities can make it difficult to embrace your particularities and love them. Learning to love your particularities is not just an individual project; you need your communities—your posse—to **see** those pieces of you, to accept them, and to love all the parts of you, fiercely.

Passing It On

Unless you've done the work to understand the places where you hurt, where rejection and judgment have caused you pain, you can take childhood wounds with you into adulthood. These wounds can cause you to lash out or even surprise yourself with your behavior. Every now and then, something will step on "little" Jacqui's toes, and suddenly I'm speaking loudly, rudely, because the feeling is familiar and my wounds are still healing. Sometimes I might have no idea why I'm behaving the way I am. Sometimes I suspect I know but can't seem to stop myself. Hurt people hurt people.

Take my dad, for example. He's a smart, gregarious, fiercely loving octogenarian who remembers everything. He talks fast and has an off-color sense of humor. All my life, I've noticed how Dad's good humor can turn sour when he feels disrespected or dismissed, when someone steps on his toes or hurts his feelings. This can still happen when his adult children don't call often enough, or our presents arrive late. And his hurt has sometimes hurt me.

When Dad was a boy growing up outside Meridian, Mississippi, his father was jailed for being in the wrong place at the wrong time—near a moonshine still where some other young men were making corn whiskey. For this and other reasons, my dad's parents divorced. Shortly thereafter, his mother married an older man named Johnson and moved my young father and his sister into the house that Johnson shared with his two daughters. Johnson taught my father how to work hard and how to care for a family. For this my father always expresses gratitude. But Johnson also taught Dad how to take a beating with belts, switches, and punches. My sense is that my father worked hard over the years not to be like his stepfather. He left home and joined the air force to get away from Mississippi and those painful, violent family dynamics. But Johnson's temper is inside Dad and part of his story; it is therefore part of mine. Though I never met Johnson, the girl I was and the woman I am are both shaped by Dad's story with his stepfather, by the way Dad was loved and not loved—all of that is in me. It made me fierce, it made me a lover, and, in order to avoid Dad's anger, it made me work **super** hard to be good.

I can count on two fingers the times I got into trouble as a child. First, when I was four, my sister, Wanda, and I decided to surprise our parents. We painted our sleeping mother's face and her headboard with her Avon lipstick samples, and then we made "coffee" for Dad by collecting snow and mixing it with grounds on the kitchen stove. The smell of burnt coffee can take me right back to the spanking that ensued, and I've never purchased Avon lipstick!

The second time I got into trouble, I was five. That time, Wanda and I "read" a giant medical book that had been stored out of reach, and that our parents had forbidden us to touch. I climbed up on a table, got the book, and we spent an hour looking at the most horrific color pictures of blisters, boils, and burns. For that, we were spanked with such enthusiasm that being good became my organizing principle from that day forward. I behaved, I didn't talk back. I bit my tongue a lot, and until I went to college, that strategy worked. But on my eighteenth birthday, my "be good" plan went a little sideways.

I was home from Northwestern University for the Memorial Day holiday—and for my birthday, which always falls around the long weekend. As usual, we were going to have a doubled-up barbecue party, but because I was turning eighteen this was going to be an extra-special day. I had always been the protector/**comadre** of my four younger siblings—Wanda as well as three younger brothers—and missed them while away at college, so I was thrilled to be home.

While we were all doing chores to prepare for the party, Wanda seemed to be getting on my father's last nerve; in his eyes she couldn't do anything right that day. I felt he was riding her too hard. I was one quarter away from completing my first year of college and loved what I was learning in psychology. This gave me the confidence to stick up for her with my newfound vocabulary. Sitting at the kitchen table where I'd been peeling potatoes, I calmly told my dad that if he continued to be harsh with Wanda, she was going to end up looking for "fathering" somewhere else. I felt so grown-up sharing my thoughts in this way, but Dad didn't welcome my input. He told me to shut the hell up, that I had no right to tell him how to raise his children since, he added, I wasn't even getting good grades in college.

I'm not sure what came over me. Perhaps I'd stored up resentment and anger while I was being good and keeping quiet all those years. Surprising the heck out of myself, I said: "Shut up? You're going to have to **make** me shut up."

The air went out of the room. It was as though things were moving in slow motion. Standing there and listening in disbelief, Wanda, Mom, and my brothers were horrified that Miss Goody Two Shoes had taken sassy to a dangerous new level. All hell broke loose! Eyes wide open, foaming at the mouth, looking obsessed, Dad lunged at me. He knocked me off my chair and pounced on me. Mom and Wanda jumped on Dad to pull him off me; he pushed Mom and she went flying. Terrified she was hurt, and hurt myself, I called my dad a name I will not write here. He lunged at me again. We were locked in a contest: Dad trying to choke me, me prying his hands off. Mom and Wanda— now standing nearby, fearfully—were screaming, my little brothers were crying, Dad was cursing.

Finally, my mother found her voice. She shouted at my father to get off of me, and this seemed to snap him out of his rage. Breathing heavily, Dad said, "Pack your shit and get the hell out."

Luckily, my best friend, Rosie, lived around the corner, and she and her mother gave me shelter when I showed up. To help me redeem what had not been a terrific birthday, Rosie's mother let us drink a glass of wine. The next day, she drove Rosie and me—we were college roommates and struggling chemical engineering majors—to Evanston to finish the quarter. She drove back a few weeks later to bring us home for the summer. Dad was still angry; no way was he driving up Lake Shore Drive to pick up a mouthy child. Sadly, this meant Mom wouldn't come, either. Once home, I apologized to Dad, but things remained very tense between us all summer. Of course, he didn't apologize but instead said, "If I hit you, it was because you deserved it."

I understand now that no one deserves what happened to me that day. At the time, however, I was thrown by the violence into a season of confusion and self-doubt. Dad's effusive love and support had been a constant in my life, even if it had always been conditioned on obedience. I was a Super Child and did all the right things, including being truthful and standing up for what is right, as I had been taught. But in a flash, I now understood that speaking truth was not allowed if it meant telling Dad something he didn't want to hear.

The more I've studied psychology, the more I understand my dad and his story. I understand that how we are loved is as complicated as the one who loves us. Dad grew up in a complicated family system, which caused him to struggle to love himself. Today I can imagine the little boy who endured beatings and who heard the kind of thing he said to me—**you deserved it**—from his stepfather. I imagine him believing that being tough was an act of strength. Still, my dad's violence scarred me, it left a hole in my self-love tank. It's part of the story that causes me to overfunction, to be "super-good," to the detriment of my health and peace. Today, in some ways, I'm still responding to being knocked off that chair.

By virtue of age and interdependence, all children are effectively held captive in adult spaces, vulnerable and unable to care for themselves. My dad was trapped in such a space when he was a child and, in turn, so was I. Hitting children, yelling at them, and shaming them damages the environment in which we raise them. Shame becomes part of their story and makes it difficult for them to develop self-love. Sixty nation-states think I'm right about this and have made corporal punishment illegal. So does the American Academy of Pediatrics.

Yes, children need to be disciplined, to be taught, to be given boundaries. But if we want to raise generations of revolutionary lovers, equipped to love their neighbors as they love themselves, we need to be creative about how we teach our children. In the classroom, on the playground, in houses of worship, or at home, too many children feel unsafe, undervalued, unlovable. They are taught—overtly or implicitly—that they are unworthy of love, which makes loving others difficult, if not impossible. Corporal punishment is one way they learn this. Being neglected, ignored, or abused yields the same result.

When I pick up the story of my eighteenth birthday and reflect on the ways my siblings and I were disciplined, I can see the wounding that was passed on to us. On the outside, the Lewis children look shiny and great. Among the six of us (I have an older half brother who was away in the army that holiday), we have a Grammy Award–winning singer who owns several businesses, an educator who writes and produces plays, and a law review attorney—a partner in his firm—who produces concerts in Europe. We also have a social worker who helps those in recovery, a retired army general who owns a leadership firm, and me, a pastor and public theologian with a PhD. Our parents loved us and gave us more than they could ever imagine: college, music lessons, art, sports, travel. As is true in every family, though we were raised by the same two people, my siblings and I each have **different** parents. Each of us experienced Mom and Dad in a unique way. I'm not sure how they would tell their stories. But when we're together, we talk about the ways we were disciplined, sometimes with the wry humor time and distance afford, and sometimes not. Speaking for myself, I know that the violence in my childhood at times made self-love a challenge, and outward success sometimes masks a tender vulnerability within.

Making Space for Love

There is no perfect family. There is no environment free of anxiety, hurt, and wounding. There is not one human on the planet with a perfect and entirely love-filled story to tell. But together we can create safer and braver environments in which love can grow. We can create spaces of empathy, imagination, and play. In those spaces, we can look at our stories—the good, the bad, and the ugly—and find wisdom in them. We can write new stories for ourselves and be deliberate in our efforts to play them out, to rehearse them in our lives. In the kind of space I'm describing, adults and children alike can flourish, heal, and learn to love themselves more.

When I was in graduate school, in search of theory and language for thoughts I'd had for a long time, I discovered a whole school of psychological thought called "object relations." In contrast to the Freudian school of thought in which human development is seen to be all about the resolution of biological drives, object relations emphasizes the **relationships** a developing child has with the **objects**—people, things, ideas, feelings, and environments—she encounters.

When a child cries, someone comes with an object—a bottle, a diaper, a blanket, a pacifier, a teddy bear—to comfort the child. At first the child feels magical, as though she created the pacifier, and it feels like a part of her. As she develops, however, she comes to learn what is "me" and what is "not me," what she can conjure and what she cannot. This space of coming to know is what object relations theorists call "transitional space." It is a space of play and creativity that becomes the space of art, culture, and religion throughout human life.

Donald Winnicott is my favorite of these theorists. He introduced the idea of transitional space and also of "good enough care," which liberates parents from the pressure to be perfect. As Winnicott explained it, if a baby's care is inadequate; if he is constantly crying and not rescued when in distress;

if his parents are distracted because they are poor, abused, wounded; if they are distant and ignore him, those feelings also become objects inside the baby's transitional space. He will pick up those cues and internalize them. Ignored, he also won't have a mirror showing him his beauty, creativity, and value. His true creative learning self will instead be anxious, looking around for a mirror that does not exist.

It is in transitional space that my grandson Octavius learns to bite his toes, scoot around, make the earliest sounds of language, and see his mom's affirmation. In transitional space, we take our first steps and are picked up and cuddled when we fall down. We learn to soothe ourselves and play alone in this space. We learn to love ourselves in this space. We learn how to parent and to discipline our children in transitional space. Love, affection, affirmation, anxiety, violence, shame—they all happen in this space and become part of us. Our stories are formed, over our lifetimes, in this space. We are **storied** and we become human in transitional space; in it we learn we are loved and take this love inside **for** ourselves, **about** ourselves.

Our nation is the ultimate transitional space, a space for our development as a species. It is also the space in which we find our identity as a global neighbor. I want it to be a safe and brave space in which we can learn to love ourselves fiercely. If the space is good enough, the likelihood of this happening for each human being increases. If the space is filled with violence, danger, unfulfilled needs, poverty, oppression, bias, racism, sexism, homophobia—that's not a good enough space for any of us to fully learn to love ourselves. These things impinge on our healthy development; they make us fearful and uncertain, angry and anxious. Unable to fully love ourselves, we won't love our neighbors, either.

If we don't take care of the space we all share, if we allow it to be filled with the objects of violence and hatred, there will be millions of human beings who don't love themselves sitting together in classrooms or board meetings, standing in line at the grocery store or theater, competing with one another at job interviews or casting calls. And these types of interactions will begin as early as nursery school or on the playground.

The search for self-love lasts a lifetime; it's ongoing work, not one and done. There have been so many moments in my life when I've taken a refresher course on self-love. When I do, when I take the deep dive into my stuff, the story of Lisa and my parents' beautiful response sits right alongside the story of my fight with Dad: Both stories shaped me. I am that good little girl, the teen who "sassed" her dad by standing up for her sister, the activist who learned about love and justice from her parents, and the woman whose stories can cause her to wrestle with self-love. All of these stories, and more, are mine. How I flunked out of engineering school and doubted my genius, how I went on to earn three advanced degrees—all of these stories are in the space where self-love grows. In my ongoing project of self-love, **I have to own all of these stories**. I also own the responsibility to care for myself, to love myself, to protect the little Jacqui inside me and tell her what my parents told me over and over again, even if not on my eighteenth birthday: **You, Jacqui, are loved so much**. I'm to remind myself of that love, alongside everything else.

And you? You're responsible for creating the space to grow love for yourself. For turning your stories upside down, for looking at them—all of them—clear-eyed and truthfully, to find where the love is. You're responsible for being rigorously curious about how you came to be you, about the stories that formed you and the stories that formed your caregivers. What did they pass down? What did you learn from the amazing moments and the painful ones? How do you make meaning of your life? And where do you go from here? What do you want to become? How do you write the story you want for yourself, with love at the center?

You're responsible for being rigorously curious about how you came to be you, about the stories that formed you and the stories that formed your caregivers. What did they pass down? What did you learn from the amazing moments and the painful ones? How do you make meaning of your life? And where do you go from here? What do you want to become? How do you write the story you want for yourself, with love at the center?

With a Little Help from Your Friends

There are lots of ways to self-reflect. Over the years, I've had help from the most amazing, wise, patient, and brutally honest friends. Rosie and Rod, who have known me for most of my life, remind me always of the healing power of laughter. Patti has been my other mother/big sister who creates a safe place for me to rehearse my stories and helps me find new meaning in them. Michael was my campus chaplain and is now one of my dearest friends. He knows my business (help me, God!) and has been a constant source of support for decades as I've worked to get my story straight. Tom and Laura are the kind of friends who express such great curiosity about my marriage, my life; they always hold my stories with love. I've got a posse of clergy girlfriends; Felicia and Katharine are the ones I most often have a glass of wine with to hash out stories about our work, our men, our parents, and the world. Macky and Kate are two friends with whom I make accountability dates to check in on how we are getting to our dreams. Susan and Claudia host end-of-Sunday dinners where I am so comfortable I might curl up on their dining sofa and fall asleep. I am so blessed to have friends who can listen to me, tell me the truth, and hold my stories confidentially.

My best friend of all is my husband, John.

John and I became friends while working together at a nonprofit that supported religious congregations as they sought to grow and tried to navigate differences in gender, racial ethnicity, and religion. We were introduced casually by a mutual colleague, and I was immediately struck by three things: how deeply blue his eyes were; how shiny his shoes were; and how good he smelled. After making chitchat, I left his office with our colleague, then spun around on my heels and went back and asked him if he was wearing Pierre Cardin, a fragrance I recognized well from having worked in the men's department of a retail store years earlier. John says I came back to flirt with him. I'm not sure; I think I just wanted to see those eyes again.

Our friendship grew while we sought to dismantle racism through our work. It grew while we told our stories. It grew while we played tennis, talked over beers, and colluded on getting our colleagues to respect my voice at the table. John was good at asking, "What do you think, Jacqui?" We've been married a long time now, and he's still awesome at asking good questions.

Your good friends can be mirrors for you; their good questions can help you examine your stories and reflect on where you've been and where you want to go. Where will you start, or have you started already? Perhaps you'll share this chapter with a friend and make a plan to be each other's narrative doula or midwife. Make a date you can keep, go for a walk, make a Zoom/FaceTime connection. Take turns sharing your stories and chart a path together toward more self-love.

I'm also a fan of therapy and counseling. Over the years, three therapists and my pastor have accompanied me in just the right ways at the right times to help me make meaning of my stories, to see the love available even in the painful events, and to help me grow my self-love. For others, a more attractive option might be a spiritual director or a coach who can help you talk your way to healing. Walking alongside someone in grief or transition is one of the most rewarding aspects of my job as a pastor. Twelve-step programs and grief support groups are other sources for organizing your life stories toward love.

Finally, and most important, you are the expert

on your stories, the ultimate meaning-maker of your stuff. What do you really think, know, and understand about yourself and your life? How can you love you better?

These are big, sweeping, and sometimes difficult questions to answer. My personal experience—and those of so many I've counseled—is that thinking of your life as a **story in progress** is more helpful. Think of it this way:

- If your life is a book, what is the title of the book?
- What's the title of the current chapter?
- What are the titles of the chapters that got you here?
- What do you want the end of your story—the last chapter—to be titled?
- What chapters do you need to "write" to get to that final chapter?
- In each past chapter, what were the stories along the way that gave you joy, love?
- What did these stories teach you about yourself? About the world? About love?
- What were the stories along the way that hurt or wounded you?
- What did these stories teach you about yourself? About the world? About love?
- What do you love about youself, no matter what?

Throughout life, we have agency to (re)write our own story and be more of who we want to be. We can cast ourselves in these stories as resilient, as rebounding, as recovering. We can write bitterness, or we can write forgiveness. We can write rage, or we can write peace. We can write obsession, or we can write release. We can write unforgiveness, or we can write grace. We can write self-loathing, or we can write self-love. It depends on what we choose to emphasize, what we choose as the primary focus of our narrative, and what we want the ultimate fulfillment of our life story to be.

This is how we will heal our souls and the world: When you and I make loving ourselves a prime objective, this self-love will source the rest. We will see clearly how connected we are to our neighbors, and to strangers, and in the spirit of ubuntu we will all succeed together. As the Buddhist saying goes, "You, yourself, as much as anybody in the entire universe, deserve your love and affection."

While you are on your journey, while learning to love yourself in this transitional space we share, lean in. Now take a deep breath and let me tell you something: **You are your best thing; don't forget it.** This is the truth.

Chapter Two

Speak Truthfully.
It Will Set You Free.

To tell the truth is to become beautiful, to begin to love yourself, value yourself. And that's political, in its most profound way.
—June Jordan

Be truthful. This was my mother's most important commandment. If you lied, she wouldn't trust you. Don't lie, she taught, because you have to keep lying over and over again, and you might forget what the truth sounds like. God won't listen to your prayers or your dreams if you lie. Even you will be disgusted with yourself if you lie. There was no room for lies in Mom's ethical universe, no lie too small to corrupt your soul, no situation so dire or costly or risky that it merited lying. A fib was a lie, a gross misrepresentation was a lie. Stealing was a lie, because it meant behaving as though what you took belonged to you, which was untruth. No matter size or scale, no lying was allowed in Mom's world.

My commitment to telling the truth began with these lessons from Mom. Be good, be honest, for God and Mom. But over time, I've come to understand that being honest is an essential building block in my self-love. To learn to love myself, I had to gaze upon myself honestly. I couldn't love what was out of view, what was unspoken about myself in my contemplation of who I was becoming. I needed to know myself authentically in order to appreciate myself. A façade or persona is too fake to love. Just as in any relationship, lies are a prophylactic blocking intimacy. The first truth in self-love is, I am enough; you are enough. This truth refutes any lie that implies you are not.

Of course, we all deceive ourselves from time to time. Perhaps we don't want to face difficult truths, or we can't access deeply hidden truths. We've chosen not to dig out the truth because we don't really want to see it. There can be an inconvenient truth from which self-deception protects us. We can fear what the truth will show us, so we tell ourselves a false story, and we make choices—often poor ones—from the place of the lie. But when we tell the truth—about ourselves, about our experiences, about our needs—we are acting out of self-love.

Being truthful isn't just about what we say; it's about how we move in the world, how we **be**. Truthfulness means making a straight line from our convictions to what we say to what we do. While lying trips us up, the truth liberates. Energy that is bound up in hiding, pretending, and lying can be used for deep love of self and love of neighbor.

Being truthful isn't just about what we say; it's about how we move in the world, how we **be**. Truthfulness means making a straight line from our convictions to what we say to what we do.

I used to hide, to protect myself, to fit in, to not make waves. Now, I constantly ask, "What's true?" I ask that question of myself all the time and work hard to find the answer. Often, I rehearse what I'm feeling, thinking, and hoping to say with my husband, John, so that the truth I speak is given with as much kindness as possible. John gets a version of the truth that might be tangy, if you know what I mean. In the end, I may tell the truth loudly, I may wrap the truth in a bow so as not to break somebody in half, but I'm trying my very best every day to speak, write, live, and be truthful—as an act of resistance, and proof of self-love. This is my guiding ethic: For the fierce love I have for myself, I move with authenticity and integrity so as to be free. But it has taken all of my lived days—and gifts from my dying mom—to get me here.

Dying to Tell the Truth

My mom, Emma Lee Lewis, died on April 25, 2017, fourteen days after her eightieth birthday. She'd been fighting small cell lung cancer for eight years. I'm convinced that my wonderful, gracious, beautiful, brilliant, stubborn mother picked the timing of her death.

I found out about Mom's diagnosis on a warm day in May, when I was thinking about getting a cheap flight to visit her and Dad in Chicago. Mom had a special connection with each of her children. For me and Mom, it was as though she sent signals through the air to me, and I'd respond by checking in. "How did you **know** I wanted to talk to you?" she would ask. "I could **feel** you," I'd say.

When I called that morning, Mom gave me her usual peppy, "How's Jacqui today, Emma and Richard's daughter, Rev. Jacqui, Dr. Jacqui Lewis-Janka?" (Though I don't hyphenate my last name to John's, she always did, to honor this man she had come to love.) After that ritual greeting, it took only a few moments to know she was upset; it was in her voice. Mom was a reedy soprano, and her voice was pitched even higher, and tense. "Precious, I've got cancer."

Cancer. When she said it, she began crying softly. My eyes filled with water, too, and my breathing became shallow. Mom had had emphysema several years before. She'd tried to quit smoking but had been unable to put down her Winston cigarettes. She had just recently managed to quit, and now this bad news. The cancer was aggressive and already at stage 4. Her doctors would make a treatment plan, she explained, including CyberKnife, chemotherapy, and radiation.

After her cancer diagnosis, Mom went through all the stages of grief, including anger. She was angry at herself for smoking. She was angry with her body; her grandfather had smoked and lived to be ninety-four. Sad and afraid, she bargained with God and with the cancer. **I've finally stopped smoking, and I want to live. Is it too late?** She prayed all the time now, this woman who got out of her bed, knelt beside it, and had a conversation with her maker each morning. Now she prayed at the kitchen table, drinking coffee, listening to gospel music on her CD player. "Order My Steps." "For Every Mountain." "He'll Never Put More on Me than I Can Bear." She'd play her **Lion King** CD, the one I bought her when she and Dad came to the theater with me. She'd play "Endless Night" over and over, because she felt she was living in one. Although her faith promised life after death, Mom didn't want to die.

In the days, months, and years to come, Mom willed herself to live, so she could shepherd us through milestones. She waited until her older grandchildren—Jourdan and Big RJ—graduated high school and college; until the younger ones— Little RJ and Rio—turned five and one. She waited until her children got through, got finished, got hitched. She held out until Wanda married Larry, Ron retired from the army, Roderick went back to teaching, Rodney became a partner in his law firm, Richard got his diploma, and John and I finished our book on multicultural churches.

She waited for her eightieth birthday, and the party she knew she'd enjoy. She waited for the menu she wanted—salmon and prime rib— and for the coconut cake with eighty candles. She waited to see the lavishly decorated ballroom filled with people she loved. She waited to get dolled-up (Mommy loved to dress up!), for the dancing, for the movie we made about her life. And perhaps she also waited to have a moment of truth-telling with each of her children, with anyone in her life who needed that kind of moment with her. I desperately needed a reckoning with Mom, so the truth would set me free.

The day after her birthday, Mom had a near-death crisis and was hospitalized. This time she had a

Do-Not-Resuscitate order. She and Dad were both suffering from her suffering. This meant she was in hospice, this meant her days were numbered. I traveled from New York to Chicago to spend time in her hospital room, reading, watching her sleep, unless she was watching me.

Mom, what are you doing?

I'm watching you.

Why aren't you sleeping?

I don't want to miss seeing your face.

You know my face.

I want to memorize it, you're beautiful.

You are too, Mommy.

Do you know how much I love you?

I do. Do you know how much I love you?

Yes, but I love you more.

Our words were in a loop, tumbling out over and over again. This was what it was like to be with her, to watch her watching me, to catch her face in the eerie blue glow of her room, to pull out the sofa bed and make it up again. To hear her cough, to use the tool to suck the phlegm out of her mouth. To fight with doctors and nurses about feeding her, hydrating her, keeping her comfortable.

This is what it was like to face the truth. Mom had been living and dying for a long time, but now? Now, if you looked closely, you could see her leaving. There was something different about her eyes. They were receding, closing just a little bit at a time.

They were knowing eyes, searching eyes, looking deeply into my soul, looking for something, trying to say something she was thinking but not saying. **I'm hurting. I hurt you. I love you. I'm sorry I smoked. I don't want to die. I'm afraid. I love you more, more than I can say.**

My mother was dying, leaving us, leaving me. And while she was dying, she was giving me something to live with. She was birthing me some more, liberating me, pushing me that last little bit out of the womb of her love. She willed herself to live until she gave it all to me. She knew I needed something—each of us needed something—but I knew best what I yearned for. It was her blessing, her understanding, her permission to be fully myself, to be a grown woman. It was her gentle nudge for me to finish becoming me. I needed her to hold the hurt with me, so we could let it go. It was absolution for us both, for any sorrow, any failure. It was getting it straight between us, getting the feeling out of us. While plugged into noisy machines that made her life possible, Mom plugged me into her, for a little while, reconnecting to me as though through an umbilical cord, sharing air, time, and truth. She spoke words of admiration, words of understanding and grace. She helped me see myself as she saw me. It was liberating, the power of truth in the space between my mother and me. Every time Mom said "I love you more," she was saying paragraphs. I heard the implicit: She loved me fiercely; she wished she had known what I'd been through as a girl. She was sorry it happened, sorry I felt shame and blame. Before she died, Mom said explicitly what she had only implied. This was a gift I really needed.

My Particular Hurt

There's a scene in one of my favorite movies, **Good Will Hunting**, a conversation between Sean (Robin Williams) and Will (Matt Damon), that tugs at my heart every time I see it. Sean is looking in Will's psychological file, a plain manila folder that represents stories in a life riddled with pain. Will wonders if Sean has had any personal experience with physical abuse. Yes, Sean had an alcoholic father, a mean drunk. Will had a stepfather who would put a wrench, a stick, and a belt on the table and ask him to choose. Will would choose the wrench because, as he explains, "Fuck him." Walking toward Will, Sean says, "This, all this shit, it's not your fault, it's not your fault." Sean reassures Will over and over again, until the younger man breaks down and weeps in the elder's arms.

This was the truth that set Will free: The abuse in his life, the pain in his life, was not his fault. He was able to grieve, to weep, to heal in the context of truth. He could drop his defenses, own his intellect and gifts, become his authentic self in the context of truth.

Regardless of the specifics of each of our scars, we all need someone to help us see the truth about ourselves. We all need someone to walk with us through the ring of fire that leads to a new self-understanding. We all need a midwife to help us birth a new self out of the womb of truth.

This scene of pain and release is familiar to me. I think of the people who have sat in my office, telling me their stories. I think of the notes I've made afterward, stored in plain manila folders like Will's, locked away safely. My notes are scribbled on the page, but the stories are etched in my heart. The girl whose mom tried to stab her because she's gay, the boy whose father beat him with a bicycle chain for being smart, the man who found out his wife is a lesbian, the woman who spoke truth and became the man she was meant to be. The hurts may be itemized in folders, but they also continue to live—if not in bruises on the body, then as bruises on the soul.

My own file is stuffed with unpleasantries, too. The pages in my file tell the story of being raced by Lisa, adjusting to military moves, and being bullied for "talking like a white girl." There's also that awkward growth spurt, when I grew six inches in the summer between eighth and ninth grades, and the humiliating, month-long menstrual cycle

I had at the same time that baffled my parents and my pediatrician.

The one that hurts the most, and left me self-conscious and sexually repressed, is a bad touch story that happened when I was nine years old. An adult I loved and trusted grabbed me, kissed me, and held me captive in his arms while trying to touch me in my most private place. He was thwarted only because I found my voice and, while squeezing my legs tight, squeaked, "Please stop, this is wrong." Though he touched me only once, his gaze was all over my body for a decade, in public spaces, while others were present but did not see what was really going on. As a result, my body shut down, my trust was trashed, and the shame I felt was devastating.

I know survivors of childhood sexual abuse who hid in plain sight by overeating. I know others who asked for help, and still others who left clues for the adults in their lives by drawing pictures with sexual content or acting out the abuse in play with other children. The way I hid from the shame inside was to put on that familiar mask and cape and become Super Jacqui. I worked all the time—ironing, cooking, doing homework, watching my little brothers, and keeping my head down. I was the "golden child," pushing myself to excel at everything, to make the hurt and humiliation go away. While keeping busy, I constantly asked: What did I do to deserve this? Why won't someone see something and say something, and make my shame stop? Is this my fault? What if I tell, will all hell break loose? What if I tell, and **nothing** happens?

That man never touched me again, but I was objectified, "thingified." He watched me, stared at me, and followed me with his gaze, inappropriately tracking my movements, my changing body, my insecure, developing self. When he caught me alone, he whispered inappropriate things to me, insinuating me into his fantasy about me. Though I was a child, he intimated that we were in some nasty thing together. And because I was young, powerless, and fearful, I took all of this in. And my wounds, though not visible, were painful, and long-lasting.

Something from outside me—the touch, the way he terrorized me with stares and taunts—wormed its way deep inside and became self-consciousness, wariness, and worry about my body, my sensuality, and my sexuality. I withdrew and became cautious about what I might do to provoke or encourage him—or someone else—to abuse me. I put up a façade, I sheltered myself with a mask of shiny, sparkly perfection to deflect his gaze, and to hide my shame.

This hiding was complicated because I also feared drawing attention to myself. Be shiny but not too shiny. Be very good but keep that goodness under the radar. I was in a bind. Most important, as a growing teen, I didn't want to be sexy. I refused to wear makeup to my junior prom. For senior prom my mom insisted I put some lipstick on and also stuffed my little bralette with tissue to fill out the bodice of my dress. Medically inexplicable, my body refused to grow breasts until I was nearly thirty.

My self-consciousness was exacerbated by the "evangelical churchiness" of my childhood. It seemed the most important commandment for a girl was "Thou shalt not have sex before thou art married." If I played spin the bottle at a party, I was bad. When I kissed my beau in the car, and he told me he was aroused, it was my fault, and I was what older Black folks called "fast," a concept I found confusing because the boyfriend wasn't considered "fast"; he was doing what he was supposed to do.

Between my churchy stuff and being traumatized by the inappropriate advances of a grown man, my sexual development was stunted. That man never raped me, his hand never made it into my pants. Still, he traumatized me, right down there in my private parts, and in my soul, before my womanhood had a chance to bloom and flower and know the joy and beauty and power she possessed.

The Truth Will Set You Free

Too many children carry scars forward—from bad adults, from bad health, and also from bad theology.

One young man I know, whom I'll call Marty, was a cherubic, beautiful boy: milk chocolate brown with big brown eyes and dimples. He loved church and its messages about the power of God's love. He sang and danced his way into the heart of his community. When he was a preteen, however, his mom moved him to a predominantly white community so he could go to a better school. But in this "better" place, Marty was ostracized. Classmates shunned him for being Black and teased him for being overweight. They also made snide remarks about his sexuality; they noticed things about him that they said just weren't right and that he himself had not yet recognized. When Marty came to the truth of his homosexuality several years later, the emotional insults grew to include being shunned by his beloved church. His love was now considered a sin, an abomination.

Marty's soul was wounded, and episodes of depression soon followed. But his love of song and dance were the things that ultimately helped him speak—and live—truthfully.

He began taking care of his body—using earnings from three jobs to eat right, work out, and get fit. He also did his research: What would it look like to get to New York, to follow his dream of being an artist? Marty took a train to Manhattan, auditioned for a job to sing on a cruise ship, and got the gig. He and some of the other performers got a Manhattan apartment together and began to pool their resources in order to survive.

Over coffee, Marty once told me his circle of friends in the artistic community and in church helped him confront the taunting and theologies that hurt him—and find his inner truth and resilience. For this community of young people, the truth was that each human is awesome and worthy of dignity and respect. Guided by this ethic, Marty and his posse created a village in which, to this day, they support one another, and make art together. They use their broken parts and their strengths in service of the vision they each share for a more just society.

What about you? I'm wondering about your little person, the one inside you. Did you encounter some of these childhood wounds? If so, you are not alone. You are also hardwired to survive—which is to say, you can be resourceful, you can put out feelers for help. Compassionate adults, peers, professional helpers—they can stand with us, and stand up for us. For our part, the thing we must do to get the help we inevitably need to survive and thrive is **tell the truth.** It takes courage, really it does, to tell the truth to someone and say: "I hurt. I'm in trouble. Can you help me?" It's difficult to know whom we can trust, but there often comes a moment of truth, a moment of candor and revelation, and this honesty can set us on a path to freedom.

It's Not Easy, But It's Right

When I was five and Lisa hurt me, my parents gave me a way to face the hurt with the truth: Racism was silly. What Mom meant was that though racism is real and a powerfully evil and wounding phenomenon, the concept of race itself is a lie. This is the truth: There is only one race—human. When my dad went to the head officer on the base and demanded apologies, he was speaking truth to power. Watching and listening to my parents, I learned the power of telling the truth. But that didn't make it easy.

To be honest, it took me a long time to tell the bad-touch story. I thought someone might go crazy if I did, and someone would get hurt. Truth-telling can be a very difficult journey on the way to freedom. Even now, I'm telling my truth gingerly here. I have reconciled with the one who hurt me; he has apologized many times, and I've forgiven him. I'm telling my truth while lovingly holding the people who know this story, know the man who hurt me, and know me.

In my faith tradition, we call that **speaking the truth—in love**. As a clergyperson, I have many truth-telling strategies. Sometimes I'm gentle, needing to take good care of the one who is listening. Sometimes I've got my fists in the air while marching for the truth, for justice and liberation. Always my intention is to free up the energy that's caught in the story, to liberate myself and the other with whom I'm in relationship to find a way forward. Can we win this action? Will the politician change policy or give in to demands? Will the congregant or colleague hear my point of view, and can I hear theirs? Can I change the story in the public square in a compelling way and open eyes, hearts, and minds to new worldviews? Will John and I become stronger because of this difficult talk? Telling the truth is an act of love, an act of resistance, an act of courage. Its end is liberation, freedom, and, if possible, reconciliation. But there can be no reconciliation without truth.

———

Telling the truth is an act of love, an act of resistance, an act of courage. Its end is liberation, freedom, and, if possible, reconciliation. But there can be no reconciliation without truth.

———

I first told my story to Mom when I was twenty-two. I told her during a tough conversation about relationships. I blurted it out; the truth erupted, loudly, not actually in context. "So-and-so crossed my boundaries . . . and tried to . . . and kept trying . . ." When I shared my truth with her, the energy between us shifted. Though she was quiet,

I felt her anger at the perpetrator. It was also clear to me that she was totally surprised. She hadn't noticed anything in me that would signal the man's abuse, and she was embarrassed, upset, and disappointed that she hadn't. She felt terrible that she didn't know. She felt responsible that he was in our lives. She also couldn't imagine what the next steps might be, how we might put him out of our lives. Our lives were connected, and it felt complicated.

Over the years, we spoke of this story again and again, moving around it gingerly, trying to make sense of it. For me, the exchanges with my mom were nervous-making. I thought, but never said, **Why didn't you know? Don't moms know everything? Could I have signaled you somehow? Is it my fault you didn't know?** I was stuck there. Of course, I was angry with the man who hurt me, but it was excruciating to admit that I was also angry with my mother, this most perfect person in my life. I couldn't bear that, couldn't bear being angry with my beautiful, sweet, kind mother. So I pushed down the feelings of anger and fear, along with my sensual self, and covered them over with sweetness and a false self. Pretending to be "okay" became a part of my personality. I could never say, "Why didn't you help me?" or "That really messed me up." I couldn't shape my mouth to say, "I was mad at him **and** at you, Mommy, because you didn't know it, and when I told you, you didn't put him out of our lives."

But then, in those last weeks of her life, Mom and I spoke truthfully about the anger I had repressed for decades. In those last days, when we were alone and talking, staring at each other, holding each other, my mom made space for us to speak my truths and hers. We talked and shared beautiful and hard truths and held them together. She spoke a truth I knew but needed to hear from her: **"Here's the truth, Jac. You're not too shiny, too strong. You didn't deserve what happened to you, and you didn't cause it by being you. Precious, it was not your fault."**

It was not my fault. In her dying, my mother bequeathed me the freedom to live a full and wonderful life.

In my last visit with Mom, I also discovered how much she needed a truth as well. She needed to know that I didn't hold her responsible for not seeing what she couldn't see. The truth is, we had both been holding on to this story between us. It wasn't my fault, and it wasn't hers, either. With the truth, we set each other free!

How can I describe the lightness of being, the swelling of my heart, of her heart, the deepness of the intimacy and trust to tell the whole truth to my mom? To not hold back, in order to protect her, or protect me. To strip down before my lovely mom, in sorrow, in shame, in disappointment, in vulnerability, in the fiercest love. She held me, she stayed with me, held it with me, while together we got the story straight. We found a shared narrative, confiding in each other—this was a stunning experience. She who had been a mirror for me in my life, helping me to become me, now saw me without the mask I'd worn off and on, so as not to shatter what I thought was fragile between us. I took my mask off, and she **recognized** me. This was an ubuntu moment—because she saw me, I could exist authentically. I was blessed. My heart sang, **"Yabo sawubona, Mommy"** which means, **"I see you seeing me."**

Preaching Life in the Midst of Death

With all the grief caused by COVID-19, and Mom's death three years earlier, Easter Sunday 2020 was not quite the "triumphant holy day" celebrated in the hymns of my childhood faith; it was, instead, a Saturday-kind-of-Sunday for me. A central story in the Christian faith is that Jesus of Nazareth was crucified on Friday—put to death by the Roman Empire for instigating love and justice—and hastily buried by his friends and family before the Sabbath on Friday evening. On Saturday, they mourned while he lay in a borrowed tomb. On Sunday morning, the women who had come to care for the body discovered that the stone covering the opening of the tomb had been rolled away. They looked inside and found that Jesus's body was no longer there; he had been, according to the faith story, resurrected from the dead.

Holy Saturday, or Easter Vigil, as it is sometimes called, is that liminal space between death and life. Year after year, the faithful wait for Sunday, that "triumphant Holy day," the hymn declares, on which a dead rabbi becomes the Christ—the Messiah—of new life. But that Easter, I wasn't there, I wasn't feeling it. It's been said that preaching is truth through personality. In truth, I was stuck in the tomb, in the interstitial, in-between space, trying to write a sermon for my despairing community while I myself felt more despair than hope.

Preparing the sermon, I took a journey into the story surrounding the death of Jesus, noticing the similarities between ancient Palestine and the situation in the United States. The so-called **Pax Romana**—the Roman peace—was an ironic nomenclature for a time of discrimination, oppression, and heavy taxation for those living in territories occupied by Rome. The abject poverty of the poor in contrast to the overwhelming resources of the wealthy; the value placed on white lives in contrast to the lives of those on the margins—then and now; the fear and loathing of the stranger; the state-sanctioned violence and murder of the vulnerable. This was the context for the Easter sermon I was challenged to preach.

Further, because of the preexisting conditions

wrought by American racism, the coronavirus was infecting and killing Black and brown people faster than it killed others, with Black people dying at twice the rate of whites. The administration had failed to act on warnings and advice given in January about the virus—warnings that, if heeded, could have saved thousands of lives. Under his assumption that the virus had come from a Chinese market, POTUS fanned the flames of racism against Asians; in March, a nineteen-year-old in Midland, Texas, stabbed three members of an Asian family in a department store. These two narrative streams—ancient Palestine and twenty-first-century America—merged in my preaching imagination. But I wasn't sure how to preach hope. How was I to preach life after so much death? Could I, who valued truth like air, be honest about my despair?

Wrestling with words for weeks, I decided to preach from Mark's gospel, the second one in the New Testament but the oldest one. As he tells the story, the women who found an empty tomb rather than a dead rabbi didn't leave rejoicing. They left the scene afraid to speak, as I'd felt many times in the past few years, fearing that our very democracy was in the throes of death. What would it mean to admit that I was afraid, that I was speechless? Could I be vulnerable in the pulpit? If I were going to do this, speak the plain truth on Easter Sunday about my speechlessness and my doubt, I knew I'd need the spirit, softness, and strength of my mom to get through the sermon. I conjured her up, she who was my first spiritual advisor and pastor.

Mom was my pastor that day when, at age seven, I took communion—the ritual bread and cup served in congregations that evoke the Shabbat meal of Rabbi Jesus—for the very first time. I sat close to her and took comfort in her familiar smells: Jergens lotion and Wind Song perfume. Mom whispered a little sermon to me. The cubes of bread came by— a sweet, Hawaiian bread—and she said softly, "This bread means God will always love you." When the little cups of grape juice were passed, Mom whispered, "This cup means God will never leave you."

God will always love you, God will never leave you, no matter what. This was not just a sweet memory for me, but proof of life, **proof for life.** It gave me words to share with my congregation that Easter morning. Without making assertions about resurrection and new life I didn't feel I could make truthfully that day, I invited my community to envision with me how life exists **in the midst of deadness.** That Easter, I couldn't say that life is stronger than death. But I **could** say that I had proof that **life is present in death.**

When a nurse sat with a dying man during the pandemic, when a hospital worker walked by the rooms of the dying and prayed—this was proof of life. When a physician left her toddlers at home to go care for the sick day after day, this was proof of life. When volunteers collected personal protective equipment (PPE) for the folks who worked in bodegas, this was proof of life. Even on a Saturday-kind-of-Sunday filled with grief, there was so much life in the midst of death. I could speak to that truth, without hiding my doubt or exaggerating my own wobbly faith convictions. Amid fear and sorrow, mourning and anger, this simple scripture in 1 John resonates: God is Love. Love was and is present in the living and in the dying. I could confidently proclaim this truth: **Love will never leave us**.

Revolutionary Truth

The historian Howard Zinn wrote, "The most revolutionary act one can engage in is to tell the truth." Indeed! I think the revolutionary part of truth is that it can free us and those around us to live with greater certainty about what is real, even when it hurts, because we are no longer shackled to the energy lying requires of us. Lying demands the continuation of the lie and the amplification of the lie to keep the truth hidden. My mom knew this. I see now that telling the truth creates ripples of authenticity that change the world.

That Easter, rather than say the words people want to hear once a year, that Christ is risen; rather than preach that God is stronger than death, I preached **God is in the death**. Neither a genie nor a life-insurance policy, God is in both the living and in the dying. You and I don't have to choose, we don't have to pretend that we are not crushed to the ground with grief when we are. We don't have to lie about our fears, insecurities, and despair. We don't have to rush to the light when the darkness is safely holding our tears, our sorrow, our anguish. We can hang out with ourselves, our posse, our Higher Power (if we have one) in between life and death. We can hover there, knowing in that liminal space there are gifts for us in between the now and the not yet.

When I think of the dying, the mourning, the grieving, and all who need a word of hope to get them through rough days, I double down on telling the hard truth rather than a comforting lie. The truth is that death is terribly hard, and sometimes life is so difficult it can take our breath away. The truth is that fear and doubt are totally understandable responses in times of crises. The truth is that it's human to lose our faith and to find it again. And if there is a God, surely God can take our leaving and returning again. The truth is that even though I'm a pastor, the God I'm most sure of is called **Love**. The truth is that darkness is all around us, and often it's frightening. It feels as though we can't escape it. But as long as we have truth, we can light our way to freedom.

I believe truth is revolutionary; it's part of the work of fierce love. Truth makes a personal, spiritual, ethical, and moral demand upon us. It wants to be said, known, told. It hurts and it's inconvenient, but it's essential to our well-being. It cleanses our spiritual palate and restores our souls. Truth is a drink of water to a parched traveler. It lubricates relationships. It liberates us from bondage. It builds trust and connections. It's the beginning of authentic living and joy. Truth eludes us at times, and we have to pursue it. Truth invites us to be honest about who we are, about our flawed-but-beautiful, broken-but-healing selves. Truth leads to reconciliation and peace; without truth, there is no peace. In the light of truth, we are able to honor our journey and love ourselves. Truth-telling is a spiritual discipline that requires practice. We must not lie to others and, as Fyodor Dostoevsky suggested, we mustn't lie to ourselves. Being honest with ourselves **about** ourselves is to love ourselves unconditionally, to love ourselves fiercely.

Truth is a drink of water to a parched traveler. It lubricates relationships. It liberates us from bondage. It builds trust and connections. It's the beginning of authentic living and joy.

Teach Your Children Well

When I was twelve, we lived in a neighborhood where children were raised by a village of parents. Boys and girls were always in our backyard, shooting hoops or jumping rope. They were in our basement, listening to music and dancing. We played board games, we roughhoused, we got into mischief. There was a boy in our circle of friends who frightened me. I'll call him Bobby. He wasn't a bad boy, but he was a troubled boy. I imagine now that he had lost a sense of power in his own family. But then, I experienced him as a kind of bully. If someone cursed, Bobby was the one to hold on to that data point. Let a child try to smoke a cigarette or sneak a kiss; Bobby was always watching, gathering stories, and threatening the rest of us. "I think I'm going to tell Mrs. Lewis that you said a bad word," or "I think I'm going to tell your momma that you tried to smoke." Each of us had something that Bobby held over our heads, each of us would plead, "Please don't tell . . . we're going to get in trouble"—because in our village you were as responsible for wrongdoing as the misbehaving child. That was the code the parents all lived by.

One Sunday, a bunch of us were playing in our basement, and this time I was the perpetrator. I snuck my dad's Richard Pryor album—the hilarious, forbidden album that I had overheard, the one that had more swear words than not—and put it on the turntable. I turned the volume down low so my parents wouldn't hear, and with hands clasped over our mouths, we laughed and laughed so hard. It was hysterical! All of us, good-ish, churchgoing preteens cracking up at Pryor's foul-mouthed comedy. When the album ended, our bellies hurting from laughter, Bobby said: "Well this goes on my list for y'all. I'm gonna tell Mr. and Mrs. Lewis first, though." And of course, we all pleaded, "Please don't tell, please . . . we'll get in trouble." And Bobby said, "Hmm, I'll see." Our little gathering broke up, everyone went home, and Wanda, our older brother Richard, and I sat down to dinner with my parents and our little brother, Ron.

All through dinner, I had a stomachache. I knew what I had to do, but it made me nervous. I had the sense that one day Bobby was going to tell any one of the stories he was holding over our heads, and when he did, the story was going to sound worse coming out of his mouth. I had to tell the truth.

While we were cleaning up after dinner, I asked Mom and Dad if we could have a family meeting. We'd never had one, but I'd heard about them, somewhere, maybe on television. Maybe they were amused. Maybe they were worried. Maybe a little of both, but they agreed to "meet." Before **The Ed Sullivan Show**, Mom, Dad, Wanda, Richard, and I all sat in the living room. And I opened my mouth and let it fly. I told them about the Richard Pryor album, I told them about the smoking, the kissing and cursing—without naming names, of course. I let it all hang out. Wanda's eyes were as big as saucers, Richard covered his mouth in surprise, and my parents had to suppress their laughter. When it was over, Bobby had no more power over us. Mom said: "This is what you wanted to meet about? Smoking is bad; even though we do it, children should not. All children kiss and all children curse. It's part of growing up. Thanks for being honest about the album; that's for adults, not you. When you tell us the truth, it makes us proud of you." Dad said, "That's right, and I'll tell you something else, the truth will set you free. Now, that's enough of that; let's watch the show." He was right: I suddenly felt free.

All truth-telling won't end with a family gathered in front of a Sunday-night television show. Some truth-telling will put you in difficult situations; it might hurt someone's feelings—maybe even your own. But in the discipline of fierce love, being honest is a spiritual practice to cultivate. You can't love what you don't fully see. Looking honestly at yourself and moving in the world with truth is critical to self-love. The truth will liberate you to be a fierce lover in the world, with you as the first object of that love. It will activate your fierce love superpower. What is unsaid is still true, it's just hiding in the dark. The truth will set you free.

Chapter Three

Travel Lightly. Downsize the Burdens You Carry.

We are not responsible for what breaks us, but we can be responsible for what puts us back together again.
—**Archbishop Desmond Tutu**

After discovering that chemical engineering was not my strong suit, I switched majors to business, and transferred from Northwestern to Bradley University. While at Bradley, I fell in love with a man named Paul. We met while serving on the dormitory staff together, at a retreat designed to get all the leaders talking to one another and creating policy. Why the two of us stayed up all night talking by the fire, I'm not sure. Why his eyes were dreamy, why his skin was creamy, why his touch on my arms—a very light touch grazing my biceps—felt like draped silk, I'm not sure about all that, either. Why the first time we kissed made me feel like melted chocolate all down to my toes, I have no clue, but that is what happened. We dated for two years, we fell deeply in love, and three weeks after we graduated from Bradley—and before we both took jobs with Eastman Kodak—we got married.

Being married to Paul was like being in a romantic comedy. Long walks in the moonlight, eating out in the artsy part of Rochester, New York. Making friends with other young couples. Driving to the Finger Lakes to see the leaves change. Playing tennis and golf. Going to the movies, walking out of the theater, and buying two more tickets to go back in. Sitting in front of the fire, holding hands, telling secrets. Sitting in the kitchen, chopping things, cooking dinner, sipping a glass of Chardonnay. My first lover, Paul taught me about pleasure, about laughing in bed, about foreplay that lasted all day long. I was so happy, we were so happy, until we weren't. When we were newlyweds, Paul and I survived a car crash. But in our seventh year of marriage, our relationship came tumbling down.

Carrying Heavy Baggage

Sometimes it's hard and painful work being human. Many of us carry our pain around like bricks in a suitcase. It's a heavy load to bear, but it's ours.

We've become used to it, so even though it might break us we drag that suitcase around. It becomes part of our identity, until we don't know who we are without it. I was carrying some heavy stuff when I married Paul, no kidding. I'd been carrying it for so long, I'd forgotten what lightness felt like. That was me, carrying around bricks as if I needed them to build strong bones; as if I needed to carry them to do penance for being me. I'd put one down sometimes, after a good conversation, or a good cry, but then I might pick up another one, to restore equilibrium. Of course, at other times, someone put the brick in my suitcase, whether I invited them to or not.

Like that time when Dad yelled at me for dating Paul, and I tried to appeal to his higher angels. Didn't he know what it was like to be in love? Isn't that why he married Mom? Did love really **know** any boundaries? To this Dad said, "I married your mother because she was pregnant with you." Aw, man, that was rough. Mom had been hiding in their bedroom while we were arguing, but she opened the door on that one. "Richard, that's not **true**," she said, which stopped the conversation cold, though the news put a whole new layer of proverbial bricks on my shoulders.

Years later, they both tried to soften this blow with more of the story. Dad had asked Mom to marry him; she said no, and they broke up. She changed her mind, happily agreed, and shortly thereafter they found out they were pregnant. Dad tortured her some about the time they were apart; had she dated anyone else? The implication was hurtful and obvious, and of course she hadn't. But this news—that I was a preconceived notion—delivered for the first time with anger and malice, was meant to hurt me, and it did. It hurt me to my soul and left me wondering if I was the cause of the pain between them. They could have aborted me and moved on. But instead, they married. Once I heard this story, I began to replay every argument I'd overheard, any raised voice expressing regret, any tensions among my dad, me, and my siblings—and felt it was all my fault.

Though it hurt to hear this news, it was also like a puzzle piece clicking into place. Oh, I thought, **this** is why I feel a low-level shame all the time! As if I might have absorbed the shame my good, Baptist, girls-don't-do-it-but-I-got-pregnant mom felt while pregnant with me.

I was also carrying the kind of religious baggage you don't even know you have until you start getting rid of it. Everything about my church life seemed about what **not** to do. My folks had been hypervigilant about my virginity so I wouldn't repeat their history. I was so freaked out about their obsession that I broke up with a boyfriend because we necked in a park and I thought we might go further.

Yes, I was carrying some stuff with me into my marriage to Paul, and that's part of what had us flipping out some, after the car accident. We decided we should get a counselor to help us deal with the post-crash trauma. We spent years with a counselor who would never offer advice but would keep repeating, "I hear what you're saying, it sounds like you're having a hard time." **Really??? You think??** Now we were with counselor number two, a woman who sat behind a steel and glass desk in a red chair—red like her lipstick. Her chair was taller than ours, so each week she commanded us—from a position on high—to get real. And she seemed to understand better than the last counselor had what, exactly, it was that Paul wanted. "Tell Jac the truth," she urged. So, he did:

"Jac, I am not in love with you. And I don't want to be married to you. I want a divorce."

It took six years of marriage and two therapists, but he said it at last. And there was more: Paul thought that my family was too dramatic for him; that although I desperately wanted to have a child, he now didn't want to have one; that although he had loved me fiercely, his love was now friendly, and he wanted out. I was stunned silent.

And so, on a warm June day, Paul and I left our counseling session and went to lunch to discuss how we would separate. This man was raised by gentle, disciplined parents—Debbie and Tim— who ate three Triscuits and ten peanuts with their nightly gin and tonic. There would be no yelling and screaming, not from him. I bit my tongue while tears fell from my eyes, a silent expression of mourning. Paul reached across the table and squeezed my hand. Then he pulled out a pad of paper on which he had listed our assets. He was obviously well prepared for this conversation, prepared to break up with me and break my heart. Here, written down, were six years of life: Golf clubs I had given to Paul; a Wurlitzer upright studio piano he had given to me; my wedding ring; our three-level raised ranch house and its furniture; two cars; boxes of photos shot on Kodak film acquired with our employee discounts; china from our wedding registry; books and record albums. We would split these things evenly. We would keep our own clothing, of course, but everything else—including the friends we had in common—we would divide in half.

I moved out and bunked with friends—some folks in my Rochester posse—waking every day in a frilly white guest bedroom with a headache from crying myself to sleep. I'd take a long hot shower and drive to work, depressed and defeated. I shied away from colleagues, moving through my workday like a zombie. I still loved Paul deeply. Our therapist said it was miraculous that we had lasted six years, given how different we were. Still, I suspected that if my family wasn't dramatic, if our parents had been more supportive, and if we hadn't crashed the car, maybe we wouldn't be divorcing. At least that's what I imagined at the time.

I was devastated and needed some distance, so I requested a division transfer, packed up my stuff, and joined Kodak's Copy and Business Product unit in Santa Clara, California, to sell high-end copiers in Silicon Valley. Though the Bay Area was beautiful, though the clouds encircled the mountains like leis on a long neck, though the deep-blue ocean was beguiling, I had the blues.

From the Bottom Up

By taking this job, I had exiled myself, far from Rochester and the man I loved, far from my family in Chicago. In time, I began to both work hard and play hard with my new colleagues. We played tennis and golf and went gambling at Lake Tahoe. We also found great recreation in alcohol, wining and dining our clients over lunch, and finding happy hours in every part of the Bay Area. My preferred poison was a Debbie and Tim classic: gin and tonic, with a lemon twist. Two did the trick.

Increasingly, it became harder to find meaning in selling copy machines. At the urging of my manager, who had noticed my funk, I started reading the Bible again, but it didn't bring the meaning I needed. He also suggested I see a counselor, but I didn't follow up on that.

Every Friday night, like clockwork, I called Paul.

From phones in bars all over the Bay Area, I told him I loved and missed him. He reminded me he loved me, but as a friend. It was a cruel ritual I imposed on myself. I kept hoping I'd get a different answer. Finally, one night I did. Paul and I talked about reconciling. He did still love me, he said. Maybe those feelings could grow back into romantic love.

Paul planned to come see me on a weekend that was exactly seven years after we'd married, and right before our no-fault divorce was finalized. He would fly in, rent a car at the San Francisco airport, and drive south to my place for a visit. I was eager to see him. I cleaned my apartment, dressed, and waited for his arrival. And waited. But he didn't show. I rationalized that his flight had been delayed, but as the minutes turned into hours, I knew something was wrong.

There can be a pain in your heart that is hard to describe, a pain that takes your breath away, that leaves your mouth slightly agape with shock and sorrow, a bitter taste drying on your tongue. You wish you could vomit with this kind of pain—the heaving would be cleansing—but it doesn't come. This was the way I hurt that evening.

I called Paul in a daze, hoping he was not hurt, expecting that he wouldn't pick up. But he did.

"Paul? Where are you?"

"I am here in Rochester, Jacqui."

"Why?!? Why didn't you come?"

"I just couldn't come. It's not going to work."

My head was throbbing, so I went to the medicine cabinet for a bottle of Tylenol. I took a couple while struggling to make sense of this hurt. Paul didn't love me anymore. He had **said** that, and I had kept calling him anyway, with gin-induced courage. I had continued to pursue him, wanting somehow to make it right again, to repair what was broken, humiliating myself, adding a brick or two to an already heavy burden of rejection.

I was angry, and I wanted to hurt Paul. While only partly listening to him, I took half the bottle of Tylenol, four or five pills at a time, and gulped them down with water. I kept thinking, **See what you made me do?** I was so weary of the pain, I poured more pills into my hand. Then I heard something; it was quiet, but persistent. Some part of me was saying,

Are you really ready to die because this man doesn't want you? Are you ready for your mom and siblings to hear that you died by taking some Tylenol? Are you ready for your dad to know that the white man made you kill yourself? Get off the phone, call an ambulance, and grow the fuck up!

I remember interrupting Paul and saying: "I have to go. I just took some pills and I have to go to the hospital." I hung up and dialed 911. The woman who answered my call told me to get my ID and sit outside on my steps, and she kept me on the phone until the ambulance came. When I got to the emergency room, they made me drink a nasty cocktail of charcoal, and I went to sleep after emptying my stomach of the black coagulation, the pills, and the vile taste of hanging on to broken shit. It all had to go.

I met with an ER doctor the next morning, and before I was released I asked for the name of a therapist. I called as soon as I could and scheduled an appointment for the next business day.

Midwifery

I found the first-floor office in Los Gatos, in one of those every-city-has-them strip malls. The glass and steel exterior did not do justice to the warmth inside. The lobby furniture was in blues and corals, there were watercolor paintings on the wall, along with Georgia O'Keeffe photographs, and magazines on the teak tables near four comfortable waiting chairs. Doc, as I came to refer to him, was an older Swiss-German gentleman with thinning gray hair and round, wire-framed glasses. His eyes were bluish green and twinkled with generosity and intellect.

We shook hands, and went inside his office, also blue and coral, inviting like the sea.

"Why are you here?" he asked with kindness, when we sat down.

I told him that I had tried to kill myself. That I really didn't want to die but wanted to punish Paul for hurting me.

"Are you feeling suicidal right now?" he asked.

"I don't want to die, if that's what you're asking. I want to live. I want to be whole."

"Then let's work on that," he said.

And we did. In our earliest conversations, Doc helped me to see that because of my past, there was a part of me that I kept hidden, a part I protected. It was through Doc that I came to understand that I had been hiding my needy, vulnerable self with my Super Girl guise. But at this point in my life, I was desperate for that part of me to come out of hiding. His hypothesis was that because I was so ready to be liberated, to live truth, I took the pills to quiet the voice of the false Jacqui, to put her to sleep, maybe even put her to death. Faced with actually dying, the truest part of me wanted to live. That's why I made the call that saved my life and brought me to Doc's office. Our shared project was to liberate my true self, so I could live authentically.

It still rings true for me today that by calling 911 and finding Doc, I was answering something genuine inside myself. It's as though a little version of myself was inside me, sitting at a desk with her hand raised, waiting to be called on. By taking care of myself, I acknowledged her, maybe for the first time. Little Jac was saying, **We are not okay. What are we going to do about this?**

Doc helped me help the little one inside me and lighten the load of the brick-filled bag I'd been carrying around, a bag too heavy for little

Jac or the adult me. Doc and I worked together
to look closely at the bricks, and the stories they
represented, and listen to what they were saying,
teaching, and showing me. We looked at my magical thinking related to my birth story and clarified
how, for better and for worse, I was not responsible
for my parents' relationship.

We also examined the bricks that represented
my missing childhood: how the fact that I was caring for my siblings at age nine made me feel both
special and also as if no one cared for me; that being
a parentified child had scarred me in more ways
than one. Doc helped me see that while I hoped
to raise a family, I would never be a good parent
until I was parented by my folks, that I needed to
go back, pick up this part of my story, and have the
holes filled with parental support and nurture. He
recommended that I reach out to my parents and
give them a chance to show up in new ways,
and that I be honest with them about the fact that
I needed their care.

Even today, as I write this, just remembering the
feeling of having to tell the adults—people tasked
with raising me—that they had not given me what
I needed makes me hurt all over again. But I did it. I
dug deep, and over several conversations and many
tears, I was able to come clean with my parents about
how abandoned I felt by them—as an overfunction-
ing nine-year-old who needed parenting; as a teen
who was afraid to disabuse them of the idea of my

perfection and so didn't show my true self to them. With Doc as midwife, I birthed a pattern of traveling to Chicago at times my siblings wouldn't be there, or I'd get there early for holidays, so I could have my folks all to myself. Though the impetus for it was difficult, Mom and Dad loved this **Jacqui time**, when we shared old stories and created new ones. We laughed a lot and also shed tears through painful memories, healing tears that made us all feel lighter. Then I would bring all of that back to California, to Doc, who helped me make sense of it.

On one visit to Chicago, I wondered aloud if they were smarting from my divorce from Paul as much as they had from my marriage to him. Mom said: "We only want you to be happy. We're sorry it didn't work out with Paul, sorry we weren't more supportive."

I was speechless. But here it was, something I pushed for, something I prayed for, something I got, finally, to help me heal. My folks and I were on the move from our parent/child dynamic to a friendship that only deepened over time. I delighted in giving them a nickname my siblings adopted, "parental units." Mom and Dad were becoming part of my posse now.

Letting Go

Almost a year after Paul stood me up, he had business in the Bay Area and asked if we could meet. We had

only spoken a few times in the interim; curious, I
agreed to see him. He came to the townhouse I now
shared with my close friends from work. When he
came to the door, we hugged. After some chitchat-
ting with my girlfriends, Paul and I were left in the
living room together. Paul moved from his chair
to sit on the couch next to me. He apologized for
hurting me, he said he knew he should have called
to say he wasn't coming to California the night I
took all those pills. While we sat, we clasped hands,
an old intimate habit from tough conversations in
the past. At one point, Paul stopped talking and
looked at me intently.

"You look really beautiful," he said. "You look
fit. Your legs look a lot stronger than they used to."

"I **am** a lot stronger than I used to be. At the
places I was broken, I'm stronger." I was strong
enough to try on new behaviors, to see what fit
me, what made sense for me; strong enough to get
help, and to get up from my depression and get out
of my house and go to work. I was strong enough
to face myself, my fears, and my confusion about
the dynamics of my faith as a young single person.

I was strong, but I had to resist Paul with every
part of myself. With him sitting next to me, old
feelings of love and desire were stirring. A part of
me wanted to have a happy ending and put our
relationship back together. But deep down in my
soul, I knew nothing good was going to come of
connecting now, because our relationship was dead.

So I gave him a strong, passionate kiss at my door as he was leaving, put out the lights, and went to my room and slept. Of course, I was still grieving over him, still loving him, but it was time to move on.

When my divorce was final, I shied away from dating at first. I put my energy into group hangouts with my colleagues—playing sports, eating out, dancing. In the clubs in the Bay Area, I was amazed at the ways Blacks, whites, Asians, and Latinos all mingled together; this was such a different experience than the all-Black clubs on the South Side of Chicago or the white ones in Rochester where Paul and I had partied together.

I went on a few dates with guys I met at the clubs, but very few resulted in second dates and none developed into anything serious. I mostly took some time for myself, still getting over Paul. I also hadn't found a church to attend and was trying to figure out what God wanted from me, what I wanted for myself, and if those would be the same things.

One night, while out for dinner at a favorite restaurant with my roommate Lisa and her boyfriend Jim, I looked up to find a gorgeous Black man staring from the table next to us. After we whispered about him some, and with only mild protest from me, Lisa and Jim invited him to join us. He gamely obliged. His name was Jonathan, and he told us about his work for NASA. An African American astronaut, in town to spend some time at Fort Ord, he was tall, bronzed, **hot**, well built, and, it became apparent, smitten with me. Jonathan charmed us all, engaging us in conversation, making us laugh, while keeping his eyes on me the whole time. The flirting was intoxicating, hypnotic. I felt that heady combination of fear and delight, that same belly sensation I loathed and loved when riding on a roller coaster; terrified, I would always get back in line for a second run. Here, too, I was nervous, excited, and hooked.

As dinner wound down, Jonathan reached for my hand, turned it over gently, and ran his fingers along the lines there, as though reading my palm. Gently stroking my hand, he looked deep in my eyes but directed his comments to Jim.

"Jim, I want to be honest here. I am a married man, married but separated from my wife. We've been separated for three years. We have one daughter, and our divorce will be final in about six months. I have never cheated on my wife, I have not had sex with anyone during our marriage. But tonight, tonight I want to take Jacqui to bed with me. I will treat her well, and with care. I will make love to her if she wants or hold her close all night. What I want to know is, do you think I can ask her to come to my hotel with me?"

Now, I was twenty-nine years old. No one had ever looked in my eyes and made me melt like that. No one had ever expressed such blatant desire. Jonathan was already making love to me, had been doing so all evening. There was a stirring in me that I recognized as my own longing. Jim and Lisa were listening intently, like parents evaluating a suitor determined to have their daughter. Jim swallowed hard, looked at me, and said:

"Jacqui, this man wants to take you home with him. What do you want to do about that?"

I said: "I think I want to go. Jonathan, where are we going?"

"I'm staying in the hotel next door, and it would be my honor if you would come with me. We don't have to do anything, or we can do everything. Will you keep me company tonight?"

Wow! There is **no way** I should have said yes to this, not me. Not the girl who taught Sunday school when she was ten and was on the church board at sixteen. Not the woman who had made love (my first sex ever) with her fiancé two weeks before the wedding, awkward, full of nervous energy and guilt. Not Emma and Richard's daughter, who had been taught that sex belonged in marriage, that making love outside of that covenant was committing adultery, and a way to hell. Not the woman trying hard to believe that her car accident and her divorce were not somehow punishments from God.

But I did. Jonathan and I went to his hotel after Jim, Lisa, and I made sure that we all had his name and proverbial rank and serial number in case he turned out to be some monster. When Jonathan and

I got to his room, we sat on the sofa in the living area of his suite and talked for hours. As the night sky lightened to greet the dawn, Jonathan said:

"Jacqui, it is time to go to bed now. Do you want to sleep out here, or do you want to come to bed with me?"

I leaned in, kissed him softly, and said, "Please take me to bed with you."

What happened next was like a sacred ritual. Jonathan ran a bath for me, washed me, and dried me. He anointed me with the small bottle of lotion provided by the upscale hotel. I waited in bed while he showered. When he joined me, fragrant with the same minty soap he had used on me, his tender kisses and kind eyes held me in the softest, warmest space. Everywhere he touched tingled with energy and warmth. I was totally comfortable; he was like a salve, or maybe even a salvation. Right at the place where I was hurting, in my heart, he was injecting a healing agent. We made love until the sun rose, and I fell asleep in his arms.

After breakfast and a shower, Jonathan drove me home. We wrote letters for a little while—short, sweet affirmations of the special night we shared, and then, suddenly we didn't. The letters memorialized the magic, making it concrete and real. It was just the right thing, just the right healing, for just the right moment in time. And we both moved on.

Our night together began a journey from a place I needed to leave to a place I needed to go, to developing my own ethical code for how I would be in the world. Maybe I was leaving "be good" and headed to "be good enough." If you're thinking, "What kind of preacher is **this** lady?" I'm telling the truth on myself. In my youth, when I should have been appropriately sexually curious, I was scared, burdened, bogged down. Jonathan was a kind of midwife to my emerging-but-not-quite-formed self. Connecting with him helped me to lighten my load, to embrace my authentic good-but-not-perfect self, to own the messiness of becoming.

My messy journey started before I was born, in Mississippi, with a little girl named Emma and a little boy named Richard making their way through their lives, carrying bricks of their own; learning, loving, leaving the South; making plans and babies; doing the best they could, almost always, with what they had. My journey is about all of the things, every story, all the moments that helped develop my superpowers **and** the heavy stuff in my suitcase. All of it led me to open that bottle of Tylenol, take too many, and dial 911.

That's why I'm here.

Finding Our Superpowers

Your life is a string of events, a collection of stories, some of which gave you irreplaceable lessons about how to live truly, stories that developed your superpowers. Even the painful stories, the ones from which you need healing and rebirth, those stories and experiences etched something significant on your soul. There's no question that the places where you have been bent at odd angles and the places you feel broken, are spaces in which you can grow strong.

And, though they can seem impossibly heavy, if you lift up your unexamined stories, your unforgiven wounds, and the crippling weight of oppression, and pay attention to what lies beneath them, you can discover the best of what it means to be alive. You may be surprised by the ways your stories help you discover the resilience of the human spirit, by the ability you have to survive the most devastating hurt and pain, and by the wisdom your wounds have for you and for your posse. Your weighty stories will also become lighter to carry once you have examined them and squeezed lessons from them. My experience proves this. So does Ben Stern's.

You may be surprised by the ways
your stories help you discover
the resilience of the human spirit,
by the ability you have to survive
the most devastating hurt and
pain, and by the wisdom your
wounds have for you and for your
posse. Your weighty stories will

also become lighter to carry once
you have examined them and
squeezed lessons from them.

Ben Stern was born in Warsaw in 1921, but his parents raised him in another Polish town, Mogielnica. After he finished college, Ben moved home to help with the family liquor store. One day, a demonstration in town changed their fate. "Don't buy from the Jews," is what the local priest had encouraged in his sermons, sending the demonstrators into the streets and away from Ben's family store. During the Nazi occupation of Poland that soon followed, Ben survived two ghettos and nine concentration camps, including Auschwitz. His family did not; he lost his mother, his father, seven brothers, and a sister.

Ben's too-common Jewish story is chronicled in the Holocaust Encyclopedia. But what happened to him next jumps off the pages for me—a shining example of the power of the examined life. Ben eventually married and had a family of his own. After more than seventy years of marriage, Ben's wife had to be moved to a nursing facility because of advancing dementia. Ben decided he would like a roommate and put an ad for one in the paper. A young German woman named Lea Heitfeld answered his ad. Her grandparents, it turns out, were Nazis, but Ben was not put off. Instead, as he told her, he felt that Lea was the perfect person to attach to his history, the perfect person to become part of his posse. For Lea, Ben's friendship was a rare gift. "This act of opening his home, I don't know how to describe it, how forgiving or how big your heart must be to do that," she said.

Ben sees a purpose to his survival: "I feel like it's important for the reason I survived to tell the world. We're different but we're all human, and there is room for each and every one of us in this world. It should be in harmony instead of hatred, racism. . . . We are all born; we're all going to go. While we're here, we should try to improve the world."

Ben lived the horror of the Holocaust. He lost his whole family. And yet **still** he found a way forward to embrace an unlikely friendship. Just when we can't imagine a way to lose the burden we are carrying, a way to lighten our load, a window of insight opens for us, an opportunity presents itself and we find our way to be healers and to be healed. Ben's ability to open his door to the progeny of the Nazis who murdered his family is beyond heroic; that compassion is his superpower.

What I Lost in the Fire

A year into my therapeutic relationship with Doc, I was offered a transfer to Kodak's professional photographic division. It would mean a nine-month training program back in Rochester and then an assignment to a sales territory anywhere in the country. I was ready to leave California, so I accepted the job. I spent a few weeks getting ready and making arrangements for my roommates to stay in my townhouse without me. Kodak arranged for a moving van to transport my things across the country; I would fly ahead. I packed clothing for three seasons, including my favorite hats and pumps; my bike, golf clubs, and tennis racket; my Wurlitzer piano, the one Paul gave me; my stereo and all my records; some family photos and two paintings so my dorm room at the training center would feel like home.

I boarded a plane, flew to Rochester, and began my training on making color prints, adjusting chemistry for the highest highs and lowest lows on black-and-white film, and selling products to professional photographers and printers. But soon after I arrived, I learned that the moving van, the one with all my stuff in it, was torched on the way to Rochester. The working hypothesis was that the truck hit power lines in Colorado and combusted. Everything burned, all of it melted in the heat of the fire. The only thing that survived was my black lacquer Wurlitzer piano. When I went to retrieve it, the smell of smoke was so strong it nauseated me. Still, though the wood was warped and some of the keys begged to be replaced, I squeezed it into my temporary housing with me.

I filed an insurance claim—itemizing all the things I lost in the fire, turning the stories upside down at the same time. How do you replace that coat you wore the time you and Paul went to Manhattan? How do you replace the used clubs you bought so you could learn to golf with your man? The painting you bought for youself in San Jose, California? When the insurance check arrived, I didn't feel like shopping. The fire had literally lightened my load, but I was too sad to refill it. Looking back, I can see that the fire gave me a chance to ask myself what was essential, what I really needed in order to survive. I didn't know what lay ahead, or where I would end up after my training, but I felt somehow nimbler and less constrained with less stuff. I was forced, in a way, to make a fresh start.

There was a time in my life when I would have thought God was responsible for the fire or was using it to teach me a lesson. Now it was difficult to imagine a God who would punish me for having sex or getting a divorce. Was such a deity **worthy** of my prayers? I wasn't sure, but little by little I was letting Him go, and that felt liberating. My life since college felt like one big narrative arc of losing some things and finding others: I found love and lost love; I was losing the old white man whom I thought of as God and finding God anew. I was finding a way to see myself and the world around me with new insight. This insight was a gift; it was like discovering I had a latent power. Through all of these ups and downs, I found a superpower. When I took off my mask and cape, I couldn't fly but I could **see.**

Friends, I can tell you from experience, from insight, that the heavy burdens you carry have lessons for you. They grow your muscle for self-love. You'll find you are strong, resilient, capable. Even the unforgiven hurts, bitter resentments, and hard feelings that weigh you down have stories to tell you, wisdom to offer. Your job is to feel the feelings, learn the lessons, and let the heaviness go. When I think of the spiritual practice of traveling lightly, I imagine you sorting through a trunk full of burdens, telling the truth about them, sorting them out, and letting stuff go, until your burdens fit into a backpack or satchel. You'll always have some hurt places in your soul, but the project of loving yourself is about healing, and getting lighter.

———

Even the unforgiven hurts, bitter resentments, and hard feelings that weigh you down have stories to tell you, wisdom to offer. Your job is to feel the feelings, learn the lessons, and let the heaviness go.

———

A Little Bit of Help

Fierce love has the power to transform you. You might need a loving midwife to help you give birth to a lighter you. It could be a friend, a therapist, a coach, or a member of the clergy. The space of transformation might be in a house of worship, at a dinner table, at a concert, or on the beach. Knowing you're carrying around extra burdens is the first step to letting them go. Becoming lighter, you can soar to a better self. There will likely be some tears and some laughter as you downsize your burdens.

Doc and I had to end our sessions when I moved away from San Francisco, but I've found another therapist where I live now. Her name is Lyn and she's a kind, brilliant, funny, loving big sister to me, as well as an emotional guide. She's a sprightly eighty, with gently wrinkled alabaster skin and graying strawberry blond hair.

Once, mourning the toughness of 2020—a year marked with political upheaval, racial violence, the isolation and death from a pandemic, raging environmental fires, and the fire that took my sanctuary—I was feeling very low and frankly so weighed down with grief, I didn't really know how to move forward. I kept throwing myself into work, running fast to do something about the pain. But, ever wise, Lyn said:

"Wait, stay right there. Stay where the pain is,

where the suffering is, where the struggle is. Stay there. That's where it's going to come. The insight. The knowing. The wisdom. Right there, Jacqui. It's not here yet, but it's coming. And when it comes, I'll midwife it with you. It will come, we will do it together. Just wait for it. It will come."

I was hypnotized, breathless while she was talking. Waiting with her, waiting on her, I leaned in to listen more.

Then she said, "We'll midwife it, and it will come right out of your . . . vagina."

The spell was broken, and we both roared with laughter.

Yes, that's anatomically correct. BUT, let me translate Lyn for all of us, those with vaginas and those without:

Right where you are, in the hurt and sorrow, that's right where the insight is, that's where the answer is, that's where the wisdom is. The transformation is there, the rebirth is there. And you're not alone. Your friend, your lover, your family, your helper—someone from your posse will midwife it with you. The healing will come, and you will emerge, shaped in the merciful womb of the fiercest love. The pain of birth is excruciating. But someone who loves you knows how to reach in and grab you and hold on to you until you make it through. You'll emerge lighter, less encumbered, ready for new stories, transformed by old ones.

I'm part of your posse, now, one of your midwives.

I'm here to help you love yourself unconditionally, speak truthfully, travel lightly. I want you to lay down your burdens, let go of the heaviness so you can give birth to a fierce love warrior—you! Ready, set, push!

YOU AND YOUR POSSE

I would rather walk with a friend in the dark than walk alone in the light.

—Helen Keller

Chapter Four

Show Kindness and Affection Wildly. Make Fierce Love Real.

We are not trapped or locked up in these bones. No, no. We are free to change. And love changes us. And if we can love one another, we can break open the sky.
—Walter Mosley

Years before our divorce—in fact, just a few months into our marriage—Paul and I were enjoying a beautiful drive on one of those late-September days. It was sunny, with just a hint of coolness in the air. We were driving from our home in Rochester, New York, to Louisville, Kentucky, for his cousin's wedding. The trip would take us due west and close to the Canadian border before we bumped into Lake Erie and followed its shore south. The sunroof was open, the fresh, crisp air blowing in our hair. The trees along the highway were just beginning to show a hint of the riot of color to come. With the benefit of years of perspective, I can now see what we were driving toward, and how what happened next would shape the rest of our time together.

It happened so fast: the spinning, turning, twisting, tumbling—each moment etched like a frame on film. A shiny reflection on the gray metallic paint of the car, a hail of gravel and glass on our heads, our eyes meeting while suspended upside down, his wide with terror. A scream, the sound of metal on concrete, the feeling of nausea. I thought, **We're going to die.**

Paul and I had been taking turns driving, and I had just taken the wheel. We'd quickly pressed our lips together as we passed each other on the way to switching seats. Paul fastened his seat belt, turned the radio down, put his hand on my thigh, and reclined his seat to enjoy the sun on his face. I was accelerating into traffic, reaching for my own seat belt, when I heard a loud, strange swoosh of air. The car seemed to veer quickly to the left, toward oncoming traffic. In a panic, I turned the steering wheel all the way to the right. The car responded, heading back to the gravel on the side of the road, then began a dizzying 360-degree spin, tires screeching, an eternity in a moment. My stomach flip-flopped; the car did, too. Three times. Roof, tires—over and over again. We tumbled through space in what could have been our grave, but once the car came to a stop—back on its tires—we were miraculously still alive. I was bleeding from minor cuts and my neck ached deeply, but Paul was bleeding a lot. His hand had somehow been dragged along gravel and was badly abraded.

A bus full of boys on their way to a basketball tournament pulled up beside us; the driver called for emergency help. It seemed like forever, but in a matter of moments, we were speeding to the hospital in an ambulance, my heart still beating fast from adrenaline and fear. I knew that when I got there, I would have to call our parents. Paul was seriously injured, and they would all want to know. But I dreaded making the calls, which did nothing to calm my nerves.

Paul and I had dated for two years before we married, and his parents—Debbie and Tim—had welcomed me often to their porch for G-and-T's (always served with Triscuits and peanuts); to their dinner table for steak and Valpolicella; to their pool to float in the sun. Debbie gave Paul her creamy white skin and dark hair; hers was perfectly bobbed to frame green eyes and long lashes. Tim was a bald and burly former football player with Paul's twinkling blue eyes, wide smile, and kind heart. They lived in Texas, in a colonial brick house with a red door; visiting them always felt a little like stepping into a scene of a romantic comedy set in Perfect Town.

Watching Paul with his parents and brother, I could see how he had become the person I loved. This family was progressive and kind. I hoped they loved me because I loved their son, and I loved them, too. But Debbie and Tim were products of an era, and they had concerns about Paul's choice for a bride **and** were too polite to raise them overtly. Instead, their disapproval came out as they wondered aloud if, perhaps, we were a little too young to marry. They also made oblique comments about the difficulties our children—mixed race as they would obviously be—might have growing up.

My mom and dad loved their children with a sweet-and-salty kind of affection, as thick as molasses and as briny as the fatback in Mom's collard greens. They would say, "I love you," to each of their children five or six times a day. They did everything they could for us, sacrificing their own needs so we could take music lessons, be in special programs, and have opportunities they would never have dreamed of for themselves. But they also expected obedience and allegiance to the Lewis code: honor, hard work, respect, faithfulness, and sacrifice. When we disappointed our parents, their tempers would blow up like a summer storm and then just as quickly pass, leaving us a little tossed and shaken. And it was perfectly okay in our house for my dad to quite simply lose his stuff and then take us outside to toss a football.

Except for that scuffle I had with my dad on my eighteenth birthday, I managed to avoid those parent-shaped summer storms. After all, being good was my organizing principle! I did what I was told, usually kept my mouth shut, and maintained a low profile by not asking for much. When my parents left our house for the birth of my younger brother, my mother stopped before lowering herself delicately into the car and kissed me softly on the forehead. I was only nine but was left in charge of dinner. "You can feed the children pork and beans tonight, and a salad," she said. I reveled in the way adults celebrated my independence. "I can do it; I'm okay" became part of my persona. It had been only a year since the family friend shamed me, so my mask was still in place, my good-girl uniform was clean and pressed. My parents and I bought into this dynamic. They got a responsible kid in the deal; I got to hide my shame in public.

My parents never taught their six children to hate anyone or to be prejudiced against anyone. In fact, their house was always the spot where folks of all races came to play cards, to break bread, to dance. Still, they didn't like the idea of Paul. In choosing him, I had betrayed them. I was loving an outsider, a member of a tribe that had enslaved our people, Jim Crowed our people, oppressed our people. Though my father's air force career put us all in regular contact with white folks, though we lived in a multiethnic Chicago neighborhood and I spent many a sleepover in the homes of white girls, they made it clear that this white boy was not welcome in our family. When we proceeded to get engaged anyway, my father was the Black person who hated our relationship most. Dad protested it by refusing to attend our wedding. He was so angry with me that if he picked up the phone when I called home, we had short, brusque conversations. Then he quickly passed the phone to my mother. "Emma," he'd say, "it's your daughter."

In many conversations with my folks about Paul, it became clear that choosing him felt like a rejection of Blackness—mine and theirs. Paul put four hundred years of anti-Black racism right in my parents' faces. The thought of us being in a romantic, sexual relationship made them think of enslaved women exploited by the men who owned them. How could their Black daughter willingly give herself to a white man when her ancestors had been brutally taken by their masters? Had their child—raised to decry and defy racism—somehow bought into a caste system? Was I trying to move up in power and stature by marrying white?

Paul sensed this dynamic and made a special trip to Chicago to ask my father for my hand in marriage. "I'm respecting your daughter," he said. "And we've not consummated our relationship." In fact, Paul and I didn't quite wait; we had sex for the first time on my birthday, two weeks before we tied the knot. But my father wouldn't know this, and he found Paul's intention and our stated choice to wait honorable. But fundamentally, my father was furious at the thought of this white boyfriend-turned-spouse loving on his child.

It was with all this in mind that I made the easier call first. Debbie answered and immediately heard the fear in my voice. Her first impulse was to ask if I was okay. I said I was, but added that Paul had badly hurt his hand and would be held at least overnight. I tried to explain what had happened, that I had been driving, that I was so sorry.

"Oh my God. . . . Tim, pick up the extension," Debbie said to her husband. This was about their youngest son—their baby—and Debbie wanted Tim to get the information firsthand.

"Can we talk to Paul?" Tim and Debbie asked, almost in unison.

I explained that he didn't yet have a room or a phone; I was calling from a hallway pay phone that he couldn't get to.

Determined to talk to her son, Debbie quickly started making plans to get to us the very next day. She explained that she should get off the phone to go check flights.

"Yes, ma'am. I'm sorry about this," I repeated. "I was driving and I'm so sorry."

"I'll see you tomorrow," Debbie assured me. "We love you."

Before making the next call, I checked on Paul, who had been moved to a double room on another floor while I was talking to his parents. I found him sleeping, his hand bandaged, an IV in his arm, his face glowing from the lights of the monitors. The other bed was unoccupied, which gave me hope that I might be allowed to stay with him overnight. I didn't want him to be alone. I also had nowhere else to go. But when I asked about that possibility at the nurses' station, his nurse explained that it was against the hospital's policy for me to stay if I was not admitted for treatment myself. I'd have to make some other arrangement.

But first I'd need to let my parents know what had happened. It was a Friday night, and I knew they'd be home watching **Dallas.**

"This is Lewis, hello," Dad said, like the military man he was.

"Hi, Daddy, it's Jacqui."

"Emma? Your daughter's on the phone. Here . . ."

And Dad was gone, anger blocking any connection to me. I swallowed hard and told my mother what had happened, that I was calling from a hospital because we'd been in an accident, I had been driving, and Paul was badly injured.

"Lord have mercy. . . . Rich, Jacqui had an accident," she shouted. "Pick up the phone." My father murmured something out of earshot, too residually angry to engage me even though I was in trouble.

"We're in Windsor, Ontario, just across from Detroit," I said. "Our car's a mess, but we're okay."

"Are you okay?" Mom pressed. "Really?"

I wasn't okay, not at all. But I'd been in training for years—pretending to be okay, putting on my superhero persona so as not to appear needy but, instead, independent and strong. So, I lied.

"Yes, ma'am, okay. A little shaky, but okay." I was biting my lip, tears filling my eyes.

"I love you," my mother whispered, as though she didn't want Dad to hear her. "I'm praying for you."

Her voice was soft, like my memory of her lips on my forehead as she left to give birth to my brother, as she'd soothed me so many times before—through skinned knees, broken toys, dead goldfish. Soft was what I needed then, standing at the pay phone in the hospital, not anger. Looking back on that young woman, standing alone so far from home, I can see how much I needed help.

I told my mother I loved her, too. And then I hung up, my head throbbing, tears beginning to fall.

As all children do, I disappointed my parents every now and then. But in the main, the contract my parents and I had—our tacit agreement—was that I would be the good big sister, the comadre to my siblings, the nice girl. In exchange, I got lots of praise. The message? Jacqui is smart, kind, important, mannerly, loving—damn near perfect, really. But in this moment, my father—and the sensitive boy inside him—continued to deny me his love.

My father continued to hold his grudge. My mom prayed. I wept.

Chicago is four hours from Windsor, yet my parents didn't come to see about me. They didn't come because Paul was white, and they were angry that I married him. They didn't come because American racism had hurt them, and by marrying Paul I had hurt them, too. They wounded me; their abandonment hurt every bit as much as the neck injury I sustained in the crash. It would be nice to write that I think they were doing the best they could, but that wouldn't be honest. I have known too many young people whose parents rejected them, put them out of doors, turned their backs on them. Whatever the circumstances, whatever the reason, parental shunning does deep damage. I find myself thinking about parenting and what it would mean for parents to love their children—even when they are disappointed—with the fiercest kind of love. That's what I needed when I crashed my car.

The Tale of Two Strangers

I wasn't quite sure what I was going to do, but right then I had to do something to take care of us; Paul needed me. Debbie was coming to us tomorrow, but how were we going to get home? I called the insurance company, and their response was wonderful. I could get a replacement car while they investigated the accident, and we could drive the rental home to Rochester. I would go to the insurance company's office when it opened in the morning, complete some paperwork, and things would go from there.

Paul and I had taken a little cash out of our account for the trip, but we had already spent most of it on gas and food. We didn't yet have credit cards, and all this was pre-ATMs. It turned out there was a branch of our national bank in Windsor, so I would need to go there when it opened in the morning, withdraw money, call a taxi, and get to the insurance office. Then I'd get Paul out of the hospital and drive us safely home. If I could get through the night, I could take care of us.

Reviewing the plan I'd made, I suddenly felt as if my knees couldn't support me. Hungry and tired, I began to really sob, salty tears stinging the tiny cuts on my face. I was feeling sorry for myself, sorry for Paul. I was used to figuring things out, taking care of my siblings and sometimes my parents along the way. But in that moment, I felt overwhelmed and sad. Paul's mom was on the way; my parents were not.

I looked up and noticed a woman standing nearby. I don't know how long she'd been watching me, but I noticed her now. She was petite, with light brown hair in a pixie cut. She had brown eyes and was wearing a lightweight black cloth coat, a flowered dress underneath, and black flat shoes. She had a kind, inquisitive face.

I tried to pull myself together as she walked closer. She told me her name. Though I remember her face, her clothing, and our conversation almost verbatim, her name is curiously lost to me. She asked if I was okay, and just the way she said it opened up something in me. It was like permission to be honest, to take off my mask and cape and show her my true self. I began to cry again; from way down in my soul, the crying came. My body hurt, my feelings were hurt. In between gulps of air, I spat out the story of our accident and the terrible feeling of being alone. She was so present to me, listening closely, making space for my pain. When I finished speaking, she hugged me, and I remember thinking that I was ruining her coat with my tears.

"How can I help?" she asked. This was such a simple question, and so hard to really answer. My mind raced with the logistics. I needed to get to the insurance company in the morning, but I also needed a place to stay since I couldn't stay with Paul at the hospital. I voiced my needs just to get them straight in my mind, not because I thought this woman would help me meet them.

Why would she? I was a stranger: not a Canadian—as it was safe to assume she was—but an African American stranger in a strange land. I must have been a sight to behold. Tall, skinny, wearing a large afro, likely with little pieces of glass in it. Small cuts on my face, jeans dirty from sitting in the gravel on the side of the road, Paul's blood on my denim jacket. There were other people in the hospital lobby, a couple of people in line at the help desk, a few families sitting in clusters on the sterile-looking, beige leather-and-chrome furniture. One of the families was Black. No one else approached me, no one else asked about me. Not even the nurses taking care of Paul had asked about how I would survive until he was released from the hospital. But this woman did. Who **was** she? What was she doing right before she crossed my path? Was she there to visit someone? Was her beloved up in a room suffering, healing? Was she an off-duty nurse, or a physician? A social worker?

I have no idea who she was or why she spoke to me. But she showed up for me and she extended wild kindness. She offered to let me stay at her house overnight and promised to drive me to the insurance company in the morning. I couldn't let her do this—I was both wary of and overwhelmed by her generosity—so she suggested she drive me to a hotel instead and come back for me in the morning. Because the bank was already closed for the evening, she said she would cover the hotel room and I could pay her back tomorrow.

I could hear her talking, I could hear her offering this incredible generosity to me—a willingness to share her time and her funds—and I was stunned into silence. There was something about this kind soul that caused her to cross the lobby to me, step over all that was unknown about me, and come into my life to help me. Startled, I could only think to lead her to Paul's room to introduce her, to share with him the kindness she was giving us. He was as amazed and as embarrassed as I was to accept her offer to help.

Yet her wild generosity only grew from there, and the details stay with me still today. She took me to a drugstore, where she bought me a toothbrush, some toothpaste, and aspirin. She took me to McDonalds and bought me a hamburger, fries, and a vanilla shake. She took me to a Quality Inn and paid the bill. She walked me to my room, watched as I opened the door, and hugged me in the doorway. Waiting for me to lock myself in, she called through the closed door: "I hope you sleep, Jacqui. It will be better tomorrow."

I turned on **The Jeffersons** to keep me company while I ate, then I took a shower and got under the covers, the room cool to my still-damp body. I stared at the ceiling for a while, thinking about my parents and Paul's, wondering about this woman's extravagance. I grew up in the church, so of course she reminded me of the Good Samaritan, who is found in the Christian scriptures, in the Gospel of Luke.

The way the parable goes, Rabbi Jesus is talking to a religious leader—a lawyer—about what it means to be faithful. Together, they review the Jewish scriptures: The way to live right is to love

God with everything you have and love your neighbor as yourself. Looking for a loophole, the lawyer wants to know who qualifies as a neighbor. Jesus answers by telling a story about a man who was robbed, beaten, and left for dead by a marauding gang. A priest and another religious man walked by and, seeing the man on the ground, they did nothing. In fact, they crossed the street to avoid the injured fellow. But a Samaritan—a mixed-race person considered in ancient times to be an impure enemy of the Jewish people—did not cross the street. Instead, he tended to the wounded man. He cleaned his wounds, took him to an inn, and paid the bill. He even told the innkeeper that if there was more owed at the end of the man's stay, he—the Samaritan—would cover the expense. The moral of Jesus's story is that the despised Samaritan is the good neighbor.

Making New Rules

In using **this** story to answer his companion's question about the definition of **neighbor**, Rabbi Jesus was getting to what he considered to be the essential laws—love God with all you have and love your neighbor as yourself. He tells the story to make the point: What you think is outside, God has put inside. The Samaritan is more inside the boundaries of what is good/pure/loving than the passersby (religious leaders no less!) who did not stop to help the bleeding, beaten man on the street. In telling this story about a hated, mixed-race Samaritan doing a good deed, Jesus is disrupting the idea of borders and boundaries. If you want to know what love looks like, Rabbi Jesus is saying, here it is: Love crosses borders and boundaries; it makes new cultural rules; it cares for the stranger. Love turns strangers into friends. Fierce love is rule-breaking, border-crossing, ferocious, and extravagant kindness that increases our tribe.

Love crosses borders and
boundaries; it makes new cultural
rules; it cares for the stranger.
Love turns strangers into friends.
Fierce love is rule-breaking,
border-crossing, ferocious,
and extravagant kindness that
increases our tribe.

In my life, I lived this parable. Paul and I crossed a literal border into Canada. Before that, we broke the rules and crossed cultural borders to get to each other, to love each other. Our parents neither appreciated nor affirmed the border-crossing; they thought it was inappropriate and dangerous. When the Canadian stranger loved me, helped me and Paul, she crossed the hospital lobby **and** all kinds of cultural borders/boundaries to get to me. She was fierce. She was white, I am Black. She was Canadian, I am American. She didn't know me, and, like the Samaritan, broke cultural rules of engagement to help me. Come to my house? Spend the night? Let me drive you to a hotel and pay? This is not what strangers do; women, especially, are taught that these kinds of behaviors are risky and dangerous. And with my little Chicago-raised self, all the rules said I should not have gotten into her car.

By breaking the cultural rules, the Good Samaritan created a new **transitional space** (from chapter 1, remember?) between himself and that bleeding man. My Good Canadian created a new space with me. She crossed the boundaries of my reticence to help me, to love me. She came all the way over to me, and I met her there. Together, we created a new system, a new dynamic, a fiercely loving space. In this new space, facilitated by a stranger, I took off my cape and mask, and I expressed my need for help. **I was new** in this fiercely loving, new space.

The Samaritan made that man on the road his people; my Canadian made me hers. When Paul and I fell in love, we became each other's people. Our parents resisted and resented our new identities, created in a new space, but they were caught up in it, nonetheless. The entrenched borders of American racism put me and Paul in a transitional space, a space for new becoming, a space our parents feared. In a way, he was now not as "white" as he had been; I was not as "Black" as my parents wanted me to be. Our parents feared this boundary-breaking space, in which we were both theirs and not theirs; we didn't fully belong anywhere. In fact, we were creating a new space in which to belong, a new border space for mixing and blending together. In Spanish this is called **mestizaje**. The Samaritan was genetically mestizaje—impure. Paul and I were culturally mestizaje; we were no longer pure enough.

This is what's at the heart of segregation. White supremacists don't want Black blood tainting whiteness. And they also don't want new ideas tainting white supremacy. Up close and personal, mixing it up in school, at work, at church, in neighborhoods—white people are faced with the beautiful humanity of the other. People of color are, too. Of course, there can be tension and conflict when we all get to the same border. But there can also be mutuality, ubuntu, shared vision, and increased strength. There can also be the fiercest love, inside which we find new kinship, new relationality.

The next morning, the Good Canadian picked me up, and took me to the insurance office, where the manager arranged a car for me to drive to Rochester. I followed her back to the hospital to get Paul. In the parking lot, I tried to express the inexpressible—my awe at her stunning generosity, my sense that some force in the universe had placed her in my life at a most tender and vulnerable time on a terrible day, and that she, in fact, had held me, and saved me.

With a tight hug and soggy kisses on the cheek, we said goodbye. I wrote to her to send her money, and we kept in touch for a while. I will never forget her generosity of spirit; her existence deeply touched my life.

Loving All the Way Home

Paul's mom, Debbie, came to Rochester the same day we drove back, to take care of him. His hand was more badly damaged than we thought; he needed to keep it elevated and his body still. Debbie got a car at the airport, drove to our house, and changed Paul's bandages and kept him company. I cooked and served the two of them. That first night, I arranged fried chicken, mashed potatoes, and peas—Paul's favorite—on our best china. I put the china on my favorite tray—wedding presents—and took it all, along with a bottle of Valpolicella, to our bedroom, where she sat vigil at his side. Once they were comfortable, I went downstairs again to eat by myself. Leaving Paul alone with his mom, I exiled myself to do penance for the accident I had caused. No one asked me to do this; this was my stuff at work. But I washed dishes and our clothes, vacuumed and dusted, all with the constant dull ache of neck pain confusing me. To my mind, being good meant putting my mask and my cape back on, taking care of Paul and Debbie, and not complaining. But deep down in my soul, I wondered: If I were truly good, if Paul and I had actually waited two more weeks until our wedding night to have sex, would that have made a difference? Was God angry with me? This question, based on bad theology, was about my residual stuff, too.

It took a few months for the insurance company to determine that our right front tire had blown out as I pulled onto the highway; that maybe we had hit some glass along the side of the road. But by then the specific cause of the accident was beside the point. Paul and I—and our parents— had made our own determinations. Paul never said it, but he communicated this for years to come: If I hadn't been driving, things would have turned out differently for his abraded hand, for his golf swing, and for us and our marriage.

In small, subtle ways, our parents seemed to agree: If we had not married, if we had heeded the cultural expectations to marry inside the racial borders and boundaries drawn at the beginning of our democracy, there would have been no accident because we wouldn't have been together that day. I overheard this sentiment when Debbie called my mom to report on how we were doing, and in the conspiratorial sounds of "Yes, we warned them, too . . ." and "This is just the least of what they have in store . . ." And even if I hadn't overheard these "I told you so"s, my parents' profound absence in those early days after the accident spoke volumes about their criticism of our choice.

Paul's hand took years to fully heal. In the haze and pain of the weeks and months that followed, we discovered that, indeed, I had a neck injury that would require years of chiropractic treatment. I tortured myself for years with questions about God and God's mercy, about goodness and purity and sexuality. I was also wounded by my father's continued cold shoulder, and, if I'm being honest, by my mother's tacit support of his position. Healing for those wounds would be a long time coming as well.

All of the people in my story, every single one of us, lived then and do now in a time when fear and hatred of the stranger—xenophobia—cause horrific violence and death all around the globe. Nothing seems as permanent and debilitating as the ways humans can hate the person unlike them. Oh, how we bear witness to this sad truth in the streets; in our political process; in theaters of war; in social media; inside bedrooms, boardrooms, and classrooms.

But there is another truth. Alongside the hurt and pain, we can see evidence of fierce love at work. My kind stranger is such evidence. People of goodwill and moral courage are crossing borders—literal and physical ones—to help one another, to heal one another. To wit: A young rabbi I know named Ari traveled to Kosovo to help get refugees to safety. Christians, Universalists, Muslim and Jewish clergy have traveled together to Ciudad Juárez over and over again to bear witness to what happens at the Texas-Mexico border, and to accompany migrant families to safety. Linda, a Palestinian American and Muslim activist from Brooklyn, invited a brilliant Zionist rabbi from California—Sharon—to offer a keynote address at the Women's March, not because they fully agree but because they love and respect each other and cross borders in friendship. Young white activists are willingly led by Black queer women in the intersectional, intergenerational Black Lives Matter movement. And in my own experience, under the banner of the Auburn Senior Fellows, I collaborate with an amazing group of religious peers—a Black Buddhist sensei, a Muslim television personality, a Sikh filmmaker, a white former evangelical church leader, and three bishops—to work for a more just society. In addition to the variety in skin tones and belief systems, some of us are straight, some are gay. No matter: Our love for one another is fierce, our collaborations born of trust and deep listening. All of this gives me hope and reminds me that love is the only force that can drive out hatred—and that it is the force that can grow a child safely into adulthood.

What Fierce Love Can Do

Amid all the outside forces at work in our culture, raising children is super hard. If you are a parent, you're present at important moments of discovery and growth all along the way, when a child is two and when she is twenty-two. You get to be wise and also glean wisdom from that person forming right before your eyes. Watch, observe, see what is becoming; celebrate the mystery of what is unfolding. Guide as best you can, to keep your child safe, while creating a brave space where they can experiment and become. Thank goodness, you don't have to be perfect; if you are simply good enough, your child will flourish right before your eyes. And your love—your **lavish, fierce love**, will surround your child with permission and confidence to be their best self. He will bask in your love; it will morph into love for his own unique and wonderful self. Your love, taken in deeply, will enable your child to stand on his feet and say, "I am enough; I am loved."

In any relationship, fierce love causes us to cross boundaries and borders to discover one another, to support one another, to heal one another. When we do this, when we go crazy with affection, and offer wild kindness to our neighbor across the street or across the globe, we make a new kind of space between us. We make space for discovery and curiosity, for learning and growing. We make space for sharing stories and being changed by what we share. This is the space of the **border**, of mestizaje, of both/and. It's the kind of space where we can enhance our knowing with what the other knows; we can develop this kind of knowing, which W. E. B. Du Bois called "double-consciousness." We can learn to see the world not only through our own stories, through our own eyes, but also through the stories and worldview of the so-called other. This is the kind of space that changes us, that grows empathy, that is ubuntu. Ubuntu is the fiercest love; it is a superpower available to all of us. We simply must open our eyes, look across the room, the street, the division, the border—and reach out to that neighbor, offering our hand, our compassion, and our heart.

———

When we go crazy with affection and offer wild kindness to our neighbor across the street or across the globe, we make a new kind of space between us. We make space for discovery and curiosity, for learning and growing. We make space for sharing stories and being changed by what we share.

———

You might not have to pay for a hotel room for a young woman in crisis, but you can be ferociously committed to the humanity of the woman in a hijab, shopping next to you in the grocery store, or walking nervously down the street. Meet her eyes, show her that you see her; that you are committed to her existence, to her thriving. Seeing her humanity, you'll never be able to think of Muslim as a category to fear.

You might not go to the border to do mission work, but there are borders right there in your community. You are on a cultural border when a group of young Black boys come your way. Their pants are low, their hats are flipped backward. Everything in your body tells you to clutch your purse and cross the street. But instead, you—like the Samaritan—stay on the same side of the street with those boys. You take a deep breath, and, like the Canadian, meet the boys where they are, and greet them with your eyes and your heart. When you see them, when they see you, you all make a new kind of connection in a new kind of space. In the spirit of ubuntu, they exist to you not as a group to fear but boys about whom to be curious. And they will see you as Auntie, as a kind lady in the village, and they will greet you right back. Over time, you might build a relationship and discover just how much they are your people, and you are theirs.

Soon, maybe there will be a shared project, some

way to make the world a little better, together. Maybe you'll support medical missions to Puerto Rico or Ciudad Juárez; maybe love will cause you to mentor children in a disenfranchised neighborhood. Maybe learning about those boys will affect how you cast your vote, and you'll pull the lever thinking of their self-interest. This connection and all the ones you make outside of the borders we all erect, they will change you and increase your love boundlessly. Sometimes you'll be the fierce lover, and sometimes you'll be the beloved; either way, you'll be changed for the better.

I'm inviting you to take some risks with me; let's get outside of what's comfortable. I want you to read different authors, listen to different music, change the channel on the news you consume, and engage with different personalities in social media. I'm inviting you to get out of bounds, to break cultural rules, to stretch what you consider inside and reduce what you consider outside and love fiercely. Why? Because fierce love goes around and it comes around. Because you can mend a broken heart with kindness. Because someone, an old Black spiritual says, "might be down in the valley, trying to get home"; you can love them all the way home.

You know what might be the riskiest, most uncomfortable, heart-expanding, border-crossing work of all? Loving those impossible people who are related to you might be what tests you most. Right there in your home, where your closest neighbors live, are folks who can get on your last nerve. Your teenaged child, who is conflicted every day about who she is, so much so that you want to throttle her. Your back-in-the-nest-again son, who can't afford his own place, who has moved in with his baby-mama and their toddler and is stretching your budget and your patience. Your spouse, who is showing you parts of their personality that make you want to pack your bags and leave. Your daughter, whom you taught to love all the people but who went crazy and married a white boy. These intimate neighbors also need to be loved. Even though you disagree with them, even though you can't fix them, when you love them across the borders of difference, when you hold them with grace, you are loving them fiercely.

And of course, you, too, deserve to be loved fiercely.

On a September evening, long ago, when I was crashing about trying to find my way, I was graciously held by a stranger who crossed borders to save me. I was tethered by a cord of kindness connecting her soul to mine. She was so very good to me. I didn't have to ask for it, perform for it, do penance for it. She showed up for me, with no history, no demands. As much as anything I've studied, as much as any sermon I've heard preached or delivered myself, the extraordinary kindness of that Good Canadian affirmed in me an unwavering belief in the bountiful goodness at the core of our humanity. I know humans have such capacity for the fiercest kind of love. When I stared into a certain abyss, that stranger healed my hurt, comforted my grief, and loved me fiercely. She helped me take off my cape and mask and be myself. She loved me all the way home—to me.

Chapter Five

Confront Boldly.
Transform Your Circumstances with Moral Courage.

> Addressing woundedness is not about blaming others. . . . Constructive confrontation aids our healing.
> —bell hooks

There is almost always a song playing in my head. My memory is full of the jingles of childhood television shows, of the jazz Mom and Dad listened to while playing bid whist, and the Motown songbook.

Music plays in the key of my joy, my restiveness, and my sorrow. It strums my pain, it shouts my hallelujahs, it begs my questions, asking, **What's going on?** Music prays my prayers when I feel 'buked or scorned, it celebrates my oh-so-happy days. It inspires dreams of California mountain rides. It drops me right into memory, mood, experiences, into laughter and tears.

I do movement-building activist work to music, worship to music, dance and exercise to music. It is one of the most important texts in my life. Music inspires me to speak the truth. Right now, Sam Cooke is singing "A Change Is Gonna Come" in my head. I memorized that song once when my brother Rod came to visit, bringing bourbon and a broken heart with him. We drank and played it over and over again, mourning a hard breakup with his girlfriend.

Cooke wrote "A Change Is Gonna Come," originally released on his 1964 album, **Ain't That Good News**, because he was both inspired and chagrined that it took a white man, Bob Dylan, to popularize a song about racism in America, "Blowin' in the Wind," and he vowed to write a song of his own. Cooke wanted his music to confront the racism in our nation, and his song to courageously call the nation to become a place of equality, justice, and inclusion.

He wrote the first draft in May 1963, after speaking with sit-in demonstrators in Durham, North Carolina. Cooke's eighteen-month-old son, Vincent, accidentally drowned in June of that year. On October 8, 1963, when Cooke, his wife, and two associates tried to register at a "whites only" motel in Shreveport, Louisiana, they were arrested for disturbing the peace. It was an excruciating year in a life pockmarked with pain and disappointment, a life that would end under suspicious circumstances when Cooke was killed months later. The song is mournful, set to beautiful orchestration. The lyrics draw us into Cooke's story, his hard life, the fear he had of the future, and his yearning that some change would come.

I understand. Confrontation can be scary, even dangerous. But if we want to transform our circumstances, we have to courageously face our fears.

A Big, Hot Throwdown

When I graduated from Drew University with a doctorate in psychology and religion, my family gathered in New Jersey for the ceremony, and we planned a celebration in New York, where I had been living. My parents drove from Chicago to Newark, then took the train to Madison. John, a dear friend from work (whom my parents had met once before when he and I had traveled together to Chicago for a conference), offered to pick them up with me at the train station. The moment we saw my parents, I could tell Dad was in a foul mood, and Mom was keeping her head down.

I wasn't sure what had happened, but obviously something had. Rather than a joyful energy at the outdoor graduation, there was prickliness, anger, and tension. It was there from the start, who knows why. Maybe Mom was slow getting ready. Maybe Dad and one of my siblings had gotten into it about something. Dad met John's offer to drive them with a scowl, the clicking of teeth, and the clucking of tongue. Was this about John? I couldn't see how, but I was beginning to wonder.

The day was so tense, there are very few photos—not of the family, not of Drew's lovely campus, and certainly not of me. Our family loves posing for pictures, but not that day. The only picture I have from the ceremony is one my brother Richard took of me, standing with my friend Traci and holding my robe. I don't look happy.

After the graduation, we all headed back to New York for the party we'd planned at my tiny Manhattan apartment. My parents would be staying with me that night. I had one bedroom, and an office, so I gave my room to them. Because the Manhattan streets were dirty, I had a "shoeless policy" and so gave my parents new slippers to wear inside. Then I hung their clothes up in my closet, put their toiletries in my bathroom, and got ready for the party.

To say Dad was rude to John would be an understatement. Dad alternately looked right through him or turned his back on him when John tried to engage him in conversation. Dad's snub couldn't have been more obvious, and I was mortally embarrassed at the slight so clearly directed at my friend. It didn't take long for John to reach his limit. He pulled me aside and told me he was leaving: "If I stay and your father keeps treating me this way, I'm going to say something to him, and he's not going to like it, and this is your special day. I'm not going to ruin this day for you, so I'm leaving." I begged him not to leave, and I continued my pleading on the elevator ride to the lobby, but John was insistent.

I stood on the sidewalk thinking, **I got a PhD today! This is my day, damn it! How many times in my life has Dad been a bully when he was angry? This has to stop!** This was now decades after our violent argument at my eighteenth birthday party. This was now twenty-three years after his clear disapproval of my marriage to Paul. I had made a new life, and with it I found a new voice. Whereas I had previously been hoarse and quiet with fear, I was now ready to speak fully. I realized the dynamic between my father and me had to change once and for all; I **had** to confront him. I took the eight flights of stairs up to my apartment, so I could gather my thoughts.

"Dad, Dad, I need to talk to you."

"What is it?" he snorted, nose flaring, jaw tight.

"My friend John just left here because of the way you treated him tonight."

"What do you mean?"

"You were rude to him, you looked past him, and you talked through him."

"Let me tell you something—"

"No, Dad, let me tell **you** something. John is my friend. When I was writing my dissertation, he was reading drafts. He was on my team working on antiracism. He supported me and stood by me while I worked full-time and wrote this dissertation."

"I don't care—"

"Let me finish, Dad. I graduated today with a PhD. You don't have any other children who have doctorates. No one else in our family does. And all day you have been salty and not celebrating with me. You didn't even want Mom to take my picture. This is **my** house, this is **my** day, and you don't get to be rude to my friends in my house on my day."

"Who do you think—"

"Dad, I am not finished. I love you and I respect you. But if you think you're going to treat me this way and stay in my life, you're wrong. I mean no disrespect, but if you disrespect me again, I will get out of your life and stay out of your life. I will see you again when Mom calls me to do your funeral. You have a decision to make."

"I don't know who you think you're talking to. And I'll tell you something else—"

"I am talking to you and I am telling you the truth. Here is why your children live far away. Here is why you sometimes wonder why we don't come around more often. It's because you are a bully, Daddy. When things don't go the way you want, you scream and holler and curse people out. Or you shun us and make us feel bad. You have put each of us out of your house at least once. Your anger pushes us away. And it's not working for me. If you want to keep behaving like that, I can't change you. You are the father and I am the child. But what I can do and what I will do is I will pull away. I will come and do your funeral. And that will be that."

My father's stunned face must have mirrored my own. My words were deeply felt, my frustration and disappointment were long held, and I couldn't believe they were finally coming out. But I couldn't hold back any longer. And it felt so right, so good, so important to confront Dad, even as it caught me by surprise.

With my chest heaving from my own anger, I said: "I'm leaving now, and tomorrow I want to talk about where we go from here. We have a day of sightseeing planned, but you and Mom can also get on the plane and go home if that makes more sense."

And I walked out the door, taking my purse and my sister-in-law, Denise, with me.

Denise is my soul sister. Her dad had been a cook in the army, and she grew up near West Point. She and my brother Ron began dating when he was a cadet; they were married at the Point when he graduated. Denise is about my height, and people say we look alike, except I am chocolate brown and she is honey-colored. We both have a wicked sense of humor, and when we're together we speak in ridiculous accents, sort of Cuban meets Brooklyn, and we collapse in laughter as we dance, sing loudly, and regress to teenage-girl foolishness. Denise has that amazing combination of compassion, joy, intellect, and kindness that made her an excellent partner to Ron as they climbed the ranks to general together.

I took Denise to a bar around the corner from my apartment. We found seats at a booth and quickly downed two apple martinis—each! I was so very drunk when we finished. But still, we went to another place I love, and had one more martini, just to make sure I passed out when I got home.

I will never remember exactly what she said as we sipped martinis in those bars, but her encouraging words and support eased the pain more than the alcohol. I was ready to sleep off my hurt, and to face my angry father and my silent mother the next morning. When we got back to my apartment, I sacked out on the living room couch and Denise took the love seat.

Mom and Dad woke early. Their padding around, the smell of coffee and bacon, and the sunlight streaming into the living room woke us up. Denise excused herself and went to shower. I greeted my parents with a warm "good morning" to break the ice.

Dad said: "Listen, we need to talk about last night. I didn't mean to make your friend leave." With this, Mom ducked into the powder room, and closed the door.

"You didn't make him leave, but he left because he was totally undone by how rude you were to him, Dad."

"I didn't mean to be rude. I saw those slippers, and I thought they were his."

"Slippers! They were **new** slippers, Dad, for you. But what if that **wasn't** true? I am grown, and this is my house. How is it that you felt you should be concerned about that?"

"He is an old white man," Dad said. "What do you want with that?"

"John is my friend. He's a minister, he's a good person. He's been a very good friend to me, and you don't get to make him feel bad in my house!"

"I really didn't mean to do that."

I clearly had momentum; I reiterated my point. "Look, Dad, you're my father, and I respect that. But this is my very special moment and you ruined it. You don't get to behave like you did yesterday in my house, in my city, on my watch. You have to respect that I am a grown woman. I pastor a church, I run my life, and I'm doing a really great job of it."

Dad said, "You're right and I am sorry," which shocked me to my core. I took a beat and said, "Okay, I appreciate that."

Mom was still in the powder room, listening and, I imagine, praying. But she wasn't coming out, not just yet.

"I love you, Dad, and I don't want to lose our relationship. But I'm not going to be able to do this with your anger and your disappointment. No kidding, I'll simply stop coming around."

"I don't want that," he said sincerely.

I pulled Dad into a hug. I heard him sniffle a little. Tears dripped more openly from my eyes. We clung to each other, for love and for life; for healing and for hope; for truth and for reconciliation. The silence made Mom come out of hiding. Calling them by their pet name, I said, "Okay, parental units, what do you want to do today?"

Mom said, "I am so glad you worked this out!"

Becoming Friends

There was still work to do, however. As it happened, my father may have seen something coming between me and John. Not long after my graduation, we started dating and fell in love. John asked me to marry him on Valentine's Day 2005. We were married two days before my birthday that year. My mom and my two youngest brothers came to the ceremony, but my other siblings had legitimate conflicts. Even after all that confrontation, truth-telling, and reconciliation, however, my dad **refused to come**, still wrestling with the idea of me marrying an "old white man."

Well, he missed a great party! Unconventional couple that we are, we had dinner with friends and family first, and then went to Middle Church for a beautiful twilight wedding, with dimmed lights, candles, jazz, gospel music, and four hundred people, including congregants and friends from our communities.

For John, I sang a jazzy rendition of one of the songs in my internal mixtape—"My Funny Valentine"—because he makes me smile in my heart. And my Renaissance man—poet, preacher, cook, consultant to congregations, father, and best friend—wrote a poem for me, which he read to a sniffing bride and softly weeping congregation. All these years later, people in my congregation still ask me for a copy of the poem.

After the ceremony, we had lemonade, champagne, and cake at the church. Then about seventy-five of us went across the street to an R&B bar and danced until dawn. My mom, my siblings, my friends, my community—my posse—all held me and John in a web of connection and love. I have a cherished photo of Mom dancing in a circle of my friends, and another of her posed with John's mom. The images of our multiethnic band of revo-lutionary lovers from all walks of life, dancing to the soundtrack we put together—the music John and I love—are etched in my memory. It was one of the best nights of my life.

I've made bad choices in my life, but John? John is my very best choice of all.

So, my best choice—the man who left my gradu-ation party so he wouldn't confront my father—decided that before our honeymoon we should go see Dad to face whatever it was that made him stay home. In advance of our arrival, Mom and my broth-ers softened the soil for the confrontation to come. They told Dad all about our art-filled wedding, the rainbow tribe of people who were there, and how much people loved John and me as a couple.

When we arrived at the house, Mom answered our knock and brought us to where Dad sat on the back patio. He was awkward, I could tell, but he stood up, shook John's hand, and gave me one of those side hugs people give when there is something between them.

After niceties, John asked for time alone with Dad, so Mom and I went into the house to cook. I learned later—from both men—that they talked about a wide range of topics that day. Dad told John stories about his childhood, about his mother, about Jim Crow Mississippi, and about the air force. John told Dad about his childhood, his life in Philadelphia, his gentle grandfather, and his racist father. They shared stories about watching the civil rights movement unfold on television, and the images of hoses and dogs turned on protesters, about what it meant to believe in freedom and justice for all people. They talked about my graduation day, the party, and how sorry Dad was for the way it went down. The rise and fall of their conversation— audible but not distinguishable—and the sound of their laughter: All of this was music to my ears.

When the sun began to set, when Mom and I were finished cooking dinner, when we went outside to get the men we loved, there had been a perceivable shift in their dynamic. Over time, Dad and John would have numerous conversations on that patio, at the dinner table, while shooting pool. They've told each other their stories, they've talked politics and culture, they've talked about raising families and retirement. They've built a relationship.

At my youngest brother's wedding, I snapped a photo of Dad and John leaning against a wall, speaking in conspiratorial whispers, and laughing. They've become friends.

Like Mother, Like Son

A few months after John and I were married, my parents came to visit us in New York. We arranged for John's feisty mother, Florence—whom we call Floss—to join us in a day of touristy togetherness. It ended with a horse-drawn carriage ride to the famous restaurant in Central Park, Tavern on the Green, where we sat outside, warmed by the early-evening sun. Dad pulled out Mom's seat before she took it, and then offered the same courtesy to Floss.

Before we even had menus in our hands, Floss took a sip of water and said, matter-of-factly: "Well, Richard, I have a bone to pick with you. You missed our kids' wedding. You missed a great party. We don't get to judge their love, you know."

Dad demurred a bit, explaining that he'd heard the ceremony and party were great. Then he looked at her directly and said, "Your son is a great guy."

"Yes," she agreed. "Yes, he is."

To this day, Dad often talks about how much he respects John for leaving my graduation party, and me for confronting him about his behavior. He also respects Floss for her direct rebuke about his missing our wedding. These confrontations set the stage for warm connections with Floss before she died in 2013—and, of course, for Dad, Mom, and John to become good friends. When Dad talks about John, he'll say: "John seems quiet, but he's really strong and he doesn't take any crap from anyone. He's just like his mother." And for Dad, not taking stuff from folks really matters.

Transformed Circumstances

Once, when my parents were driving me to the airport after one of my visits during Mom's cancer treatment, my father did something seriously uncharacteristic. As he moved the car through traffic, he asked for help. "Emma," he said, "is the exit for the airport coming up on the left or on the right?"

I had **never** heard my father ask my mother about directions. He was seventy-eight years old then, very proud and very strong. He cooked at least once every day for my mom, who was by then attached to her oxygen tank. He still worked as a substitute teacher whenever they called him in, usually two or three days a week. He was stubborn, too. He maintained his garden, even though it hurt his back to do so. And he ignored the fact that he was old enough to delegate cleaning out the house gutters or shoveling snow. As "the man," he could take care of himself and his wife, and he knew how to get where he was going, damn it.

But not today.

"It is on the left, Rich; um hmmm, you got it, love."

Wow! Asked and answered. No tension, **plus** affection. This seemed like a breakthrough. I found myself wondering who took my parents and left **this** couple in the car??

In the quiet of the car, I smiled to myself,

thinking about this couple who fell in love dancing, finding their **thrill on Blueberry Hill.** They
were just as likely to be lovey-dovey as to send
verbal zingers at each other, or to whisper in my
ear, "Your dad is getting on my nerves today" or
"You know, I love your mother, but she talks too
much." In the twilight of their lives, in the midst
of aging and cancer, they grew to love each other
more deeply, they depended on each other. Their
sometimes fraught relationship—tense from Dad's
temper—was transformed in these years. It became
warmer, gentler, and more tender as they united
to confront the cancer my mother was battling.
Whether getting ready for church or a date with
chemo, they coordinated outfits, deciding between
their favorite blue or brown palettes. Dad was
fiercely committed to keeping Mom alive; she
was committed to his living, often staying awake to
watch her beloved sleep.

Rides to the airport with my parents were always
rich with revelation. On another ride, just before
we popped the trunk to get my luggage, Dad said:
"Tell John we said hello. And I'll tell you something
else, that man has cured my prejudice. I'm not
lying. If more people were like John, there would
be no racism in the world. I am so proud of the
two of you and so happy you are happy. Tell John
to keep making you happy."

I went home to John, my sweet and tender husband, and when I told him this story, he teared up;

he was incredulous. So I called my folks and put them on the speakerphone, thinking John deserved to hear this firsthand.

"Hey, Mom and Dad, I'm home. Dad, did you say John cured you of your racism?"

"Yes, I said it. Don't get me wrong, I am a Black man, a Black man from Mississippi. I'm Black to the core. But, yes, I said it and it is true. Love y'all, goodnight."

And Dad hung up.

Confronting Is Honorable

"Honor your father and your mother" is one of the Ten Commandments, all of which my parents made us memorize (in full) as children. We learned this code of ethics, alongside multiplication tables, the names of presidents, and Black history facts.

What does it mean, now, to honor my parents? As a child and as a young woman, I thought it meant keeping quiet, not speaking up, storing up a trunkload of microaggressions, and putting on a mask to hide when I was hurt. It took time, but I've come to understand that honoring my parents also meant confronting the troubling places between us. Confronting hard things was what real love looked like. Honoring them and loving them meant using my true voice to build a grown-up relationship with them. Healing through these conflicts and confrontations has not only helped me to be me but also taught me how to be morally courageous in my life as an activist and faith leader. I'm grateful.

———

What does it mean to honor my parents? As a child and as a young woman, I thought it meant keeping quiet, not speaking up, storing up a trunkload of microaggressions, and putting on a mask to hide when I was hurt. It took time, but I've come to understand that honoring my parents also meant confronting the troubling places between us. Confronting hard things was what real love looked like.

———

My parents had the moral courage to insist on justice and fairness when it came to their children and the world around us. They were politically active, they participated in neighborhood-improvement projects, they joined picket lines, and of course they confronted our behavior when they found it offensive or objectionable. I suppose it was because of their role-modeling that I was able to find the courage to speak truth, **even to their power,** and advocate for the relationship I needed from them.

Listen, friend, I'm not saying that every time we confront something with moral courage it will transform our circumstances. Sometimes confrontation goes wildly wrong! But I am saying we must turn toward the things that need changing and try to change them. Inside our families and circles of friends, inside our posses, there can be intense pressure to keep our mouths shut and just go along. The status quo has a lot of power; even when we don't like it, it's what we know. I'm saying that confronting what is broken or harmful or evil or dangerous is the beginning of healing our souls and the world around us. I'm saying that keeping silent about what's wrong or unjust or simply uncomfortable doesn't change anything. I'm saying what James Baldwin said: **Not everything that is faced can be changed, but nothing can be changed until it is faced**. Confrontation is awkward and difficult, but if we can find the moral courage to do so, it **can** transform our circumstances. This transformation might start at home, in our most intimate and caring relationships. The transformation might begin inside of us, as we confront our ghosts and lighten the loads we carry.

Inside our families and circles of
friends, inside our posses—there
can be intense pressure to keep
our mouths shut and just go along.

The status quo has a lot of power;
even when we don't like it, it's
what we know. But confronting
what is broken or harmful or evil
or dangerous is the beginning of
healing our souls and the world
around us. Keeping silent about
what's wrong or unjust or simply
uncomfortable doesn't change
anything.

———————

I'm sure it wasn't always intentional, but my parents created a space for me and my siblings to learn how to face the difficult things, even when it meant facing **them.** Amid conflict and chaos, in spaces of apologies and reconciliation, in times of joy and celebration—I learned the art of confrontation and the value of moral courage from my folks. In good times and in bad times, for better or for worse, in sickness and in health, these old Black people became my posse. Through it all, we loved one another fiercely. I will honor them and what they taught me for as long as I have days.

You, right where you are, in the relationships that matter most to you, can create a laboratory for truthful speech, for confronting what hurts and needs to be healed, for fixing what is broken in your relationships so that they—and your soul—can feel at ease. Fierce love calls you to this, even when it is awkward, even when you are afraid. You can create the dynamics you want—by changing you!

It might take some time, but I hear Sam Cooke in my head, singing about how even though it would take a long time, the change for which he yearned was going to come. Here's hoping change comes in just the way you engender it, at just the right time.

Chapter Six

Think Inclusively.
They're Your People, Too!

God's dream is that you and I and all of us
will realize that we are family, that we are
made for togetherness, for goodness,
and for compassion.
—Archbishop Desmond Tutu

Before I made my living talking about God, thinking about God, writing about God, I was a person
struggling to have a relationship with God. I had
been given a god to believe in, some mixture of
what my parents believed, what my preachers
taught over the years, and what my imagination
made of the parts of the Bible I read. In my early
twenties, I often had more doubt than faith—
doubt in what I'd learned, doubt in what those

teachings implied for my life and for the world. I was frustrated; how is a God whose name is Love appropriated to justify violence, hatred, and enmity around the world? Over and over again, I was struck by how religion—**which means to bind together**—gave humankind license to hurt others, to put people out, to leave people behind. And yet, how does religion oftentimes inspire people to such incredible acts of generosity, kindness, and morally courageous imagination?

This chapter might appear to be about faith, but it's actually about growing up, about coming of age, about accepting a calling to the vocation of fierce love. It's about letting go of childhood belief systems that may not serve you well now. Whether political, spiritual, philosophical, or ideological, your belief system might be blocking you from the love you are called to give and receive in relation to your posse. What would happen if you laid that system down and let a new one emerge?

Whether political, spiritual, philosophical, or ideological, your belief system might be blocking you from the love you are called to give and receive in relation to your posse. What would happen if you laid that system down and let a new one emerge?

Leave No One Behind

In the summer between my freshman and sophomore years in high school, my friend Leslie and I took the two-hour ride in Rev. Brown's car to the Presbyterian church camp in Saugatuck, Michigan. Rev. Brown was the very cool, bell-bottom-wearing, afro-sporting pastor of Seventh Presbyterian Church. Accessible and irreverent, a man who rarely preached about hell and those who deserved to go there, Rev. Brown made church joyful, even for rebellious teenagers. With the windows down and wind in our hair, Leslie and I made plans to bunk together in the girls' cabin: She had dibs on the top, and I was happy to have the bottom. Her mother, Mrs. R, was one of the chaperones every year. She was a wiry, strident lady; lean and strict, but also funny and kind.

Wanda was too young to come to this high school camp-out, so my older brother, Richard, and I represented the Lewis family. The oldest kids on the trip were a couple of years ahead of us—they were rising seniors—and had been planning just how wild they would get on this camp trip for months. While we were stowing our gear on the vans that would take us north from Chicago to the still beauty of the camp, they snickered about the cheap wine and vodka they had packed in their suitcases. I overheard one of the oldest boys whispering about pills and pot, which he called reefer.

On the second-to-last night at camp, the wild-
ing happened. We had been well behaved and busy
all week, so the adults gave us some space. We
were allowed to sit on the beach, play our boom
box, and dance around the campfire unchaperoned.
As the darkest night approached and the moon
lit the lake, the older kids began to couple up,
and the slow music came on. Leslie and I sat by
the fire, watching, smiling, wishing we were as cute
as Cindy, as grown-up as Marlene. We watched as
the couples danced, as the younger boys got rowdy
with one another, as the suitcase was opened and
the drinks were poured into Kool-Aid cups, as the
pills were taken and washed down with the wine,
as the reefer was lit and passed. All this letting loose
was riveting, but it felt awkward to just watch and
not participate. Fortunately, it was close to the
eleven o'clock curfew, which gave Leslie and me an
excuse to leave the glow of the fire and head back
to our cabin.

We trudged through the sand, barefoot, on the
moonlit path to the shower room, where we washed
the beach off our faces and feet and brushed our
teeth. We made our way to the cabin that had been
our home for almost a week, arriving with ten
minutes to spare before our curfew.

I admit I felt some kind of good about being
on time, like acing the test. Mrs. R was not happy
to see us, though; she didn't exactly celebrate our
on-time arrival. She scowled and demanded to

know where the rest of the girls' cabin was. Trying to avoid tattling on the others, we said they weren't far behind, that we'd "tried" to get them to come with us but they wanted to stay a little longer. Mrs. R was furious. She lectured: "You should have **waited** for them, and brought them back with you. It's not enough that you followed the rules. You're all responsible to each other, for each other. If they break curfew, you're all breaking curfew, because they are your people."

With that, Mrs. R punished **us** by making us sit up on Leslie's bunk, backs against the wall, to wait for our posse to come to bed. The other girls showed up at 1:00 a.m., sluggish, sleepy, all partied out. They'd get their own punishment in due course, but in the short term we all got a talking-to over breakfast. We needed to learn, Mrs. R urged, that our success and our thriving were not individual projects. Our choices would impact our families and our community. In our community, we were never going to leave anyone behind.

When we had quiet time that afternoon, I spread my towel on the beach and lay down, watching the clouds move slowly across the bluest blue sky. I found myself almost hypnotized by the sound of the lake rising and falling, the sand warm under my body. I felt as if I was grounded and floating at the same time. In the simple beauty of that spot, I let Mrs. R's admonition wash over and through me. I felt peace, love, tranquility, and excitement all at once. I felt the truth of what she said deep within me.

Looking back, I can see that this moment—and her words—planted seeds in me that would eventually grow into a new theological self. Everything—my spiritual maturation, my grown-up faith, my preaching, teaching, writing, activism, and advocacy—all would become a quest to leave no one behind. Along the way, I would shed the belief system of my childhood—already in pieces—and build a wider tent for myself and others, so we would get to healing and liberation together. I'd let go of the sexuality-obsessed god of my youth, the one who demanded my virginity and obedience in order to love me. I'd let go of the god who only had room for so-called perfect Christians in his kingdom, who had punished me to get my attention. I would claim a Universalist faith, bound in freedom and love for all people, and boldly declare: "God is Love. Love. Period. Everything else is commentary." I was on a journey of calling, and transformation. But I had a ways to go.

Finding Home

When I was living in Philadelphia, after the fire burned up my belongings, I had a crisis of belonging. Twelve of us graduated from the Kodak photographic sales training program and got our territory assignments. My territory extended west from Philadelphia to Lancaster, and south to Wilmington, Delaware. Kodak's relocation program helped me sell my townhouse back in California and buy a place in Valley Forge. I added a car to my meager possessions so I could get to my customers easily. So, effectively, I was settled in. But I was lonely: I had no friends, except the now disbanded training cohort. I forced myself to have coffee with a few of my customers, and one of them, Leo, became my first friend in my new world. We went on a few dates, tested our chemistry, found we had none, and developed a warm friendship instead.

One Sunday, a few months into our friendship, Leo took me to church. Berean was a historic African American Presbyterian church in Philadelphia. The senior minister, Rev. Dr. J. Jerome Cooper, had gone to high school with Leo's mother, so my friend was able to give me a personal introduction after the service. As we stood eye to eye, it was clear to me that Rev. Cooper was one part holy man, one part rebel, and one part rascal. He had a round, brown face, and his bald head gleamed in the light from the stained-glass window directly above us. His purple robe was just a little taut across his middle, which only made him human. But I felt immediately that he could see into me as though he already knew me, and he smiled as though he were keeping a secret.

When I lived in California, I would sometimes visit churches, hoping to find a home. I'd sit near the back, watch the dynamics, sing the hymns, and hope to engage the preacher after church. I'd stand in line, waiting for a chance to say, "Can I talk to you about how you came to be a pastor?" Leo's introduction gave me more than an opening to do this now. After sharing some niceties about his sermon, I went for it. "Rev. Cooper, when did you know you would go to seminary?" I asked. "Can we talk about it?"

"Sure," he said, "let's have lunch now."

Over sandwiches in Rev. Cooper's office, I dove into the story I needed to tell. I told him about Mrs. R's admonition to leave no one behind, about my sense that the work of being a fierce love warrior was my calling.

Rev. Cooper said: "I can see your calling in your face. That's why you're here."

That's Why You're Here

"That's why you're here" was one of the most profound affirmations of my entire life. As I describe that long-ago moment, my eyes still tear up. Here was the moment of insight. Here was the **yes** I had been yearning for, the **yes** that made sense. All of the moments that put me on the path to Jerry's office now felt purposeful, set in motion so Jerry would see me, hear my story, acknowledge that feeling in me, and say, "Yes, I see it in you." In an amazingly ubuntu way, being seen as called made my calling real. I had found a home in which to begin letting go of some of the theology that had thwarted my development as a woman, in which to get whole with a posse of people all trying to find home.

More recently, I witnessed this moment from the other side of the proverbial aisle. The Middle Church board had been searching for those who felt called to become church deacons, a role that would formally enlist them as administrators of emotional and financial support to the congregation. The final candidates were five amazing laypeople who are active in our church community. They sing in the choir, make videos, raise funds, and march for justice. When asked why they decided to apply for the deacon role, each described the sensation they had when invited. One candidate, Thelma, said: "I want to serve and love my friends. That you invite me to do so means you **see** that in me." Another, Deborah, said: "I love being in this conversation, it's like I'm becoming who I think I can become because we say it out loud." These folks all experienced what I did that day in Jerry's office; we saw their gifts, acknowledged them, and helped make their vocation real.

Several of the candidates also expressed doubt

about their calling to this work. For one, it was whether she had enough experience; for another, it was whether he had enough confidence. One wondered, as I've wondered over and over again—and perhaps you do, too—if she was good enough. Like all of us, she has lived a life with ups and downs, with successes and failures. She has judgments about herself on her mind, judgments from her parents in her ear, judgments from our culture in her heart. "Yes," our interview team said to the one doubting her experience, "you are called." "Yes," we said to the one doubting his confidence, "you are called." And, "Hell yes," we said to the one judging herself against old tapes, "you can do this, you should do this."

To each person, we wanted to communicate: We are all here, struggling to live up to the values we share, so join the crowd. Join the band of everyday folks falling down and getting up again, failing, trying, often shining with compassion and kindness, sometimes backsliding into pettiness and fear. Welcome to being human. Do your best, right where you are, to love someone into healing. When you are off your game, someone else on the team will step up and do the work. This message to our new deacons is a message for you, too, dear reader. You don't need to walk through fire or pass any tests to be a love warrior. You simply say yes. That's why you're here.

———

We are all here, struggling to live
up to the values we share, so
join the crowd. Join the band of
everyday folks falling down and
getting up again, failing, trying,
often shining with compassion and
kindness, sometimes backsliding
into pettiness and fear. Welcome to
being human. Do your best, right
where you are, to love someone
into healing. When you are off your
game, someone else on the team
will step up and do the work.

———

At the end of each interview, our team raised hands in the Zoom squares in which we found ourselves that season and blessed each soul: "You are seen, you are loved, we thank God for you." This blessing was for each candidate, but also for each of us. In our ubuntu community, we are seen and loved—sawubona—by our ancestors, by the angels, by our Higher Power, and by one another.

This recognition of the other is strong medicine for thinking inclusively, for getting whole collectively. Jerry affirmed that he could see a calling in me, a purpose in me. We offered this same acknowledgment to the people who became deacons. We saw their gifts for care and support and welcomed them to use those gifts in our community, to help us make sure no one in our posse was left behind. That was their calling, why they were there.

I'm encouraging you to look in the mirror, see your face there, and hear me tell you: This is your calling, friend, to make sure no one in your posse is left behind. And look around you—all of those people are your posse, too!

Family Found

Once Jerry and the leaders at Berean affirmed my call to ministry, I joined the church. Many men were supportive and welcoming, but it was the female deacons of the church who really became my people, my posse. These strong Black women cared for the sick, counted money, taught children, cooked brunch, paid the bills, polished pews, chased away the smell of aging carpets, nurtured my calling, and healed my soul. They were clear that their mission was to heal their entire community. I had been told along my life's journey that women couldn't be pastors, but **these** women welcomed me to ministry and, in stages, to their pulpit. First, I made announcements from the front of the sanctuary, then read scripture from the stand on the side of the pulpit reserved for lay leaders. Finally, I got to sit in Jerry's chair, then stand, with my head covered—the custom at Berean church—and preach from the lectern.

That year, I preached four or five of the worst sermons of my entire career, sermons that were disorganized and repetitive, but they were received with love from my new community. Inevitably some church mother would say: "Baby, you're trying, bless your heart. And one day you'll go to seminary and have your own church." These fine people took me in as family, celebrated my calling, and increased my faith in God and in humanity. I was at home with them and therefore beginning to feel at home in my skin. I worked hard for Kodak during the week, took Saturdays off, and worked for God, Inc. on Sundays at Berean. I was tired, and happy, almost all the time.

Washing dishes after church, listening to laughter and gossip, praying with people in pain, walking on the paths near my house—this community and my neighborhood were brave and safe spaces to practice new behaviors, and to heal from old wounds. This was found family, and I was so thankful. Their love was a healing space for me.

It was Jerry who took me on a drive one day in the fall of 1989 to Princeton, New Jersey, to see the seminary there. He believed it was the only place I should go, and since I trusted him it was the only place I applied. When we arrived, we met with Jerry's old friend Geddes "Guy" Hanson, a Princeton theological legend, and toured the campus. It was—and is—a stunning place, and I knew that the verdant fields, stately brick buildings, modern media center, white chapel on the edge of campus, spacious library, and quaint, old-fashioned dormitories could feel like home to me.

After the tour, Jerry took me to the chapel basement to meet with the campus pastor, Rev. Michael Livingston. Jerry planned to leave me there, so I could privately say what was burning in my heart. I wanted to tell someone the truth. I was divorced; I was frightened that I was not good enough to say "Yes!" to God, that I was already destined to fail.

Michael is a warm, engaging Black man who is kind, intelligent, insightful, and funny as hell. He commands authority with his compassion and earns the right to tell you the truth straight to your face because he listens deeply not only to what you're saying but also to what you mean to say. I felt the truth of this in his office that first day and poured out all of my business, hardly taking a breath. I told him about my struggles with perfectionism, and the way I felt I always had to earn my place in any room. I shared my anger over my sexual abuse by a trusted family friend, and how unprotected I felt by the adults in my life who didn't see and didn't know. We talked about my evangelical upbringing and my shifting theology. Most important, I confided in him that I felt unsure I was fit to serve God.

I remember saying, with tears in my eyes: "There is no way I can live up to what I expect of myself, to what my parents expect of me, to what God expects of me. I am divorced, and I can't believe I even applied to seminary. What was I thinking?" Michael said: "You are exactly who God is calling to ministry, Jacqui. **Exactly** who God will use to help people know God, find God. God is calling you **because** of who you are, not **in spite of** who you are. You and the people you serve will get whole, together."

This was the most revolutionary notion to me. I had come to believe that organized religion was in the business of picking and choosing. Some folks were in, and some folks were out. There was a contract, tacit in some churches, explicit in others. In order to stay in, you had to keep the rules, pay your dues, and not ask any questions. If you broke the contract, you could expect that you would be put out, kicked out, left behind. Michael's idea of religion was something new: I was loved exactly as I was. I was an inextricable part of Love. Not only me, but all people, no matter how they named God or if they named God at all—we all belonged to a Love so amazing, so compelling, that if we leaned into it, we would be welcomed. That compelling Love made us all family. There was, as an old Negro spiritual claimed, "plenty good room in God's kingdom" for all of us. In fact, we shaped the love, made the love, formed the love by being ourselves.

My heart leapt, and I wept. It was the next step in a conversion process that would take more than a decade, but I was on my way.

Getting Better at Being Me

These days, I put myself in a truth-telling space with Michael about once a month: sometimes for coaching on an issue I'm working on, sometimes to dissect the social justice issues we both care about, and sometimes just to laugh at life. Once, we were talking about the theology I was carrying around in that first meeting. Michael said: "There was a spark in you, waiting to be lit, you were tinder for a raging fire to come. You needed to hear one thing and it was easy to say, 'Let that shit go. Let it go!' And you shed it so fast!"

Once I was seen and encouraged to put down some stuff and say yes to the work of love, once I heard what my whole body and spirit knew really mattered, I felt like Helen Keller when she learned how to read. I was eager, rushing, trying on new identities. I wasn't one to sit still, and not everything fit, but this is who I was, who I was becoming. I kept pushing forward out of my old theology and became more comfortable with my questions. I learned from trying on new things, growing from the learning, getting better at being me.

In my first semester at Princeton Theological Seminary, I was confronted with questions I had never pondered—most especially, just how literally was the Bible the word of God? This question buzzed around everything: from women and preaching to manifest destiny and chosenness to economic justice to homosexuality. Gay ordination was the most controversial area of all, with protests, teach-ins, resistance, and advocacy occurring on what seemed like a daily basis. Since I had no idea what to think of all this, my first question was "What does the Bible say?" And the answer came loudly from conservative colleagues: Gays are an "abomination" and "against nature."

As a Christian, I had learned only ten commandments, none of which said anything about being or not being gay. In the gospels, Jesus hadn't said anything about being gay. Puzzled, I went to the part of the scriptures these colleagues were referring to—the texts about purity codes. I read about keeping kosher, about not eating shellfish or pork, about avoiding mixed fabrics and not touching a woman during menstruation. And there, too, was the mention that a man shouldn't lie down with a man as he would a woman. But it made no sense to me that we were singling out the texts relating to gay sex while still wearing different fabrics, still engaging with women while they were having their periods, and still eating shrimp and barbecue ribs! All of this was so maddening to me. I realized that seminary was about both learning and unlearning what it meant for God to have a say in guiding human life.

My own view came into clearer focus when, at the suggestion of one of my teachers, I read a book by Chris Glaser, a white gay man my age who could not get ordained because he was gay and out about it. Reading his story, it was clear that Chris was **born** gay—thus was gay by design—and so he hadn't broken any laws! As the psalmist wrote, every human being is "awesomely and wonderfully made" just as they are. To me, this meant that if any of us are created in the divine image, my gay friends are, too. I found a sense of kinship with my LGBTQIA+ colleagues, and my heart expanded. They deserved justice, welcome, and acceptance. These were my people, my posse; I would not leave them behind.

Their stories and their struggles converted me from "What does the Bible say?" to new questions: What is the context in which the Bible says that? And does that make sense? And is that right? **And does it square with Love?** If it didn't pass the test of love, if the scripture meant leaving one of God's people behind, I was ready, as Michael had urged me, to let that shit go.

Through the Lens of Suspicion

So began a delightful season of heresy for me. I joined the resistance! I was suspicious, suddenly, that without rigorous work to explore the historical contexts of biblical texts, clergy all over might be keeping their congregants bound to a religion that was not quite grown-up, that was churlish, rigid, and judgmental. That there was collusion to keep the clergy silent and the church underinformed. That clergy and seminaries might fear that the people sitting in the pews could not handle the truth. That somehow the religion of a revolutionary lover named Jesus turned into a propaganda machine intent on leaving anyone not white, male, straight, and Christian behind.

I needed the truth like a blood transfusion. The truth of how the Bible became a bible through counsels and compromises. And I thought that the people in the pews might enjoy the truth, too. That our scripture came into being as scribes wrote down the oral traditions they assumed were inspired by God's Holy Spirit. That, of course, because the scribes were human, there must be errors in the text. That the miracle of these texts is the consistent ways they point to love and justice. That even though the Bible is a closed book, God is still speaking, and revealing God's will and way to humankind. That in order to understand what God desires for us, we have to listen with our whole hearts and with our minds. That we are called to love God with all we have and to listen to God with all we have. That rather than use religion to hurt and punish one another, it should bind us together, and heal us as one people.

Though I was a little nervous, I was excited to be in a new space with God. I felt free, liberated, and excited about what God was saying to me and to the world. What I would have previously considered blasphemy was now my responsibility; I had to question, to test, to wrestle with the words on the page and in the air. I approached my classwork with the rigor and curiosity of a convert. Gone was the red-letter King James Version of the Bible memorized and held in my mind. It was replaced with a cavernous hole, ready to be filled with something new. Doubt and faith mingled together. My faith was emerging, it was more like faith in the ongoing revelation of God. Faith in the ability to hear God still speaking. With this came an enormous gratitude that I might be one of the people charged with helping others grow their way to new theologies.

Finding My People

On a sunny October afternoon, I walked over to the cafeteria to interview with churches looking for interns. There, against the east wall, with sun shining on her face, was Patti Daley. Petite, fair-skinned, with dark brown eyes and hair to match, she was laughing when I approached. I had on one of my many hats, and she loved that I wore it to the interview. It was a red fedora, tilted just a little, and I knew it made me look fierce and fresh, a thought I cherished. Patti and I sat down to talk about faith, calling, urban ministry, and Myers-Briggs personality types. We discovered we were the same type—ENFP—extroverted, intuitive, feeling, perceivers who lead with vision and passion. This was one of many things we would find we had in common.

Patti hired me to work at Bethany Presbyterian Church in Trenton. I started an after-school program, preached, led worship, and started a jazz program outside on the lawn. I fell in love with urban ministry, with the people of Bethany, and with Patti and her family. Patti shared them with me; her husband, Eliot, and her children—Allison, Shannon, and Jad—became my people. Their living room was my sanctuary, their laughter and storytelling a balm in Gilead. Platters of cheese and charcuterie, bottles of wine, uproarious laughter—these kept me sane while I was deconstructing and reconstructing my faith.

I'm Patti's people and she is mine. Through many dangers, toils, and snares, through breakups, setbacks, and amazing changes in my life, we are each other's posse for life.

Like Patti, Michael has never let me go. Time has changed our relationship. He was my pastor, mentor, coach. Now he's my friend, co-conspirator, and confidant. He's been my people, my homie, for more than thirty years now. What an honor it is when Michael needs **me** to listen, to hear his story, and maybe even give a little advice.

When I graduated seminary, I was called to start a new church in Trenton together with a group of others who were assigned to leave their home church for three years and start a new one. We made our congregation in an old, abandoned building and we called it the Imani Community Church. **Imani** means "faith" in Swahili. Linda and Dave, Pat and Jim, Stephanie and her sister Donna, Mary and Stan, Cherry and Dave were just some of the multiethnic band of leaders who started this church with Afrocentric ethics—ubuntu ethics—and love. We became lifelong family. We loved one another as we married, divorced, married again, had children, and buried loved ones.

One of our beloved, I'll call her Beverly, was a drug user when she came to the church. She was beautiful, smart, and had the most lovely singing voice. But she was sick with crack cocaine and couldn't shake it. She had been to rehab, she had struggled in twelve-step meetings. But in our community, in our family, she found siblings, she found aunties and uncles for her children. She got clean, she relapsed, she got clean again. Once in my office, Bev said: "You know why I was able to do this? It wasn't for you or for God, it was for **me**. But I knew I could do it because this family thought I could." Bev raised her children, got a great job in the city, and is still clean and sober. She got well inside our village. And so did I. Loving those people and being loved by them filled a hole in my soul I did not fully know existed. The relationships completed something important in me.

We also found unlikely allies and friends outside our congregation, among them a group of young Black men who were part of the Five Percent Nation, which I had never heard of until I moved to Trenton. Founded in 1963 by a student minister to Malcolm X—Clarence 13 X—the Five Percent Nation derived its name from their doctrine that separates all people into three categories. Only 5 percent of whom are righteous people who understand their truth—that each Black man is the living God who can teach freedom and justice to Black communities.

The men in our neighborhood who shared this belief system were young, brilliant, badass community organizers. I didn't agree with their theology but very much appreciated their commitment to strengthening Black communities. They were as outraged as anyone at the violence and poverty in Trenton. When a call went out to our neighborhood to organize for justice and against injustice, they came with their wives and children. Together in a multiethnic coalition of Catholics, Jews, Baptists, and Presbyterians, we all worked for police reform when a young woman named Jenny was shot to death in her boyfriend's car in an arrest gone horribly violent. Together we took on the mayor, we worked to get drugs and needles out of our playgrounds and to make our streets safe. We respected one another and our differences. When I left my congregation to go back to graduate school for psychology—the next stop on my educational and spiritual journey—my allies in the Five Percenters showed up in church that last Sunday morning. With their proud, elegant women in white hijabs to celebrate me, these brave and strong men came to my multiethnic church (**that means some white people were there!**) to wish me a fond goodbye. Though we didn't agree on many things, I was their people, and they were mine.

Acceptance

My time in seminary and in Trenton were exercises in acceptance. I'm a tenacious resister; I don't give up easily, and I think giving in is overrated. But acceptance became a spiritual discipline, as I sought to shift myself and participate in my own healing. I accepted that the Bible is not literal but full of wisdom, stories, and proverbs for reflection and encouragement toward making my whole life work. I accepted partnerships with Jews, Christians, Muslims, agnostics, and atheists as legitimate and joy-filled. I accepted "mothering" from a petite white woman named Patti and from a strong Black man named Michael. I accepted that my life had been purposed so I could partner with Love and with other flawed human beings, like me, to heal our souls and some of the world. I finally accepted myself.

I also accepted this: There is nothing so special about the work of fierce love that I had to be perfect to do it. I was equipped when my faith was strong and when it wavered, and I was still equipped after my divorce. I was ready and able in my ordinariness to be a revolutionary lover, not because I was shiny but because I was loved. The ability to love fiercely and with compassion is all that is required.

There is so much evidence of an ideological war being waged not only here in the United States but around the world. Who will we be as a global community? That identity is what's at issue. Compassion, generosity, taking responsibility for all the world's children—these are some ideals that call us to fierce love. Competition, rising white nationalism, and xenophobia make other claims on us. Unexamined, our guiding philosophies might be polluted with fear, hatred, and unconscious bias in subtle and stark ways. If we examine our beliefs though the lens of fierce love, we can build an ethical and just society in which more and more people thrive. If we think of the stranger as our neighbor and ask, **What would Love have me do**, we might make choices that help us heal collectively, choices that heal our souls and the world.

You, my people, are loved fiercely and called to the work of healing. You and I, we're the ones we've been waiting for, we the people. We're called to do justice, love kindly, and walk humbly together toward a better future. We will get whole collectively, as one human family. We will make our world just and safe and fair and equitable. We will have one another's backs. We will get to the promised land, as a people, together, because together is the best way—perhaps the only way—to travel there.

YOU AND THE WORLD

An act of love, a voluntary taking on
oneself of some of the pain of the world,
increases the courage and love
and hope of all.
—**Dorothy Day**

Chapter Seven

Live Justly. Choose Fairness and Equality Every Day.

Power at its best is love implementing the demands of justice, and justice at its best is power correcting everything that stands against love.
—Reverend Dr. Martin Luther King Jr.

When I was a little girl, the only thing I loved more than flying through the air on the swing set was to watch my mom, no matter what she was doing. Sometimes that was from the vantage point of the fluffy pink toilet seat, peering up as she put on the sweet-smelling face powder that made her glow, or as she painted her lips and then kissed a tissue to blot off the excess. I loved watching her take pink rollers out of her hair. I'd cover my mouth and nose when she blasted her hair with spray meant to keep the curls in place.

I watched her in the kitchen as she made biscuits, her hands powdered white; when she used the drippings from the beef shoulder roast to make gravy for the mashed potatoes; and as she fried chicken, always careful to drain it so it would stay crisp.

I also watched my mother watch the world, and in so doing took cues on how to love the world around me. I watched her make soup for sick neighbors, stretch the food on our dinner table to feed latchkey kids, and visit church members in the hospital. Daily I was learning when to laugh and when to cry, when to mourn and when to dance, how to be a good person. Indeed, her calm, appropriately simple reaction and explanation of the racism I experienced at the hands of little Lisa in Mrs. Easley's classroom was a model for how I would come to move in our enduringly racist world. When Mom told me that night that some people wouldn't like me because I'm Black, she pulled back the curtain and opened my eyes to the racism all around me. And yet her fierce determination for me not to take the racism personally, and the way she prayed with me about it, showed me a way to deal with racism as the activist I would become. Watching Mom helped me learn how to live justly in the world, and how to make everyday choices toward fairness and equality. Watching her was like reading a book on how to love my neighbor, the stranger, and the world, as I loved myself.

White Rage and Black Grief

I mourn my mother's loss, and I miss her face—a window to her feelings, a cue for mine. I miss her especially at this point in my life when, as I write, the world continues to battle COVID-19 and has lost such a disproportionate number of Black and brown people to it. As the physical church I love has been lost to fire. As violence against AAPI communities escalates in heartbreaking ways, making the call to fiercely love our neighbors even more urgent. As an angry mob beat its way into our nation's Capitol, violently protesting an election they truly believed had been stolen from their president. As the trial of the man who knelt on the neck of George Floyd—killing him—also puts our justice system on trial, and the nation waits to find out if Black grief and Black deaths matter.

If she were here, I would tell her how damn tired I am of living in a country that treats Black grief as a threat and white rage as a sacrament. To wit: The contrast between the treatment of the Capitol insurrectionists and my own experience in the same building several years ago is stark. I was there—outside the office of Mitch McConnell, then the Senate majority leader, with a group of multiethnic leaders—to demand that the Republican-led Senate not take away the Affordable Care Act. We stood there in unison and sang, with passion but in peace. The Capitol Police were not opening barriers for us, gently pointing the way for us, nor were they taking photos with us, as some did with the mob at the Capitol. Though our protest was both peaceful and permitted, we knew that the very fact that Black people were in charge of our effort meant more potential for a police escalation to violence. We'd seen it too many times before.

In the immediate aftermath of the disturbing events at the Capitol in January 2021, many pundits wrung their hands and lamented, "This is not who we are." But in fact, it is **precisely** who we are, and who we have always been. White rage, white grievance, and white entitlement have always been privileged over Black grief, Black justice, and Black well-being. I'm saddened by the images playing over and over again on the news: Confederate flags flying, folks charging up the steps of the Capitol, breaking into offices. But these images do not represent a new phenomenon.

When I was sixteen and researching a project on racism, I saw for the first time the picture of fourteen-year-old Emmett Till's lynched body in a spread in Jet magazine. His mother, Mamie, is in the photo, too, gazing upon her son's bloated and disfigured face. One of his eyes was missing. His crime, it was reported, was that he had flirted with a white woman. I've seen the violent rage of white police officers beating marchers on the Edmund Pettus Bridge and glass ketchup bottles smashed down on the heads of students sitting at lunch counters. I have seen rocks thrown at children integrating schools. Closer to home, I saw the police viciously beat a neighbor while arresting him for outstanding parking tickets. I heard his cries, saw his head bleeding, saw their red faces, twisted in rage. It was Derek Chauvin's white rage, casually, murderously kneeling, delivering 9 minutes and 29 seconds of torture—simply because it could.

White rage is why we have the Ku Klux Klan. In response to new freedoms conferred upon Blacks after the Civil War—including the right to vote—it was white rage clothed in white sheets that terrorized Black people, hanging men, women, and children from trees, tearing off pieces of their flesh. White churchgoers watched and took pictures of some of the lynchings, holding their children on their shoulders for a better view.

White rage produced the brutal response to Black success in Tulsa, Oklahoma. It cried foul when Black students get into Ivy League schools, and it spread suspicion about the legitimacy of the presidency of a Black man with a Muslim name.

White rage turns violent when Black trans and queer people dare to walk down the street in joyful freedom; the joy itself seems to incite the rage. Chants of "Black Lives Matter" cause enraged white people to counter with "All lives matter." What they really mean is that if a Black life matters, their white life doesn't matter enough. White rage turns violent toward protesters in every generation who demand human rights, who dare to call white supremacy the lie it is.

This story of white supremacy is as American as apple pie. Thomas Jefferson himself spoke of it in his "Notes on the State of Virginia." He itemized the many ways that Blacks are not as beautiful, not as smart, not as loving, not as deeply feeling as whites, and even speculated that our grief is transient. But, oh, how wrong he was! Black grief is not transient; it is generational, incarnate in our bodies. We rap it, sing it, write about it, dance it, and take it to the streets. Yet when we do so, our grief is met with disdain. We're told to get over it.

When Black grief shows up in the office and dares to speak up, demanding that the glass ceilings be shattered, the backlash from white rage interprets that grief as "too angry." The Black employee isn't a team player, he can't be coached and therefore can't be promoted. In this way, Black grief—which of course is angry—is shut down, cut off. The result is a grief that rots, depresses, and kills our souls.

Black grief isn't transient; it is prophetic. It knows how to weep, wipe its tears, and organize for justice. It's persistent and knows how to keep its eyes on the prize and hold on. It knows that anyone who believes in freedom cannot rest until it comes, until the death—and the life—of a Black mother's child is as important as a white mother's child.

Black grief is resilient because it knows the arc of the moral universe bends toward justice and nothing is going to turn us around. Black grief finally gives way to joy because though weeping lasts for a season, joy always comes in the morning.

There are many reasons human beings fight with one another, persecute one another, and oppress one another, but race tops the list. As the psychologist Robert Carter put it, race is a **different** difference. But that also means that if we can find our way to healing on this big and thorny issue, if we can make racial justice an everyday spiritual practice, we will have changed our view of humanity and the world we inhabit. If we can disrupt racism, if we can make choices based on fairness and equality, I believe we will have cleared the way to resolving related issues like poverty, economic disparity, and environmental justice that are tied up in caste, discrimination, and xenophobia. Race is therefore worthy of special and specific focus. We must challenge the premises of our racist culture in which being Black is a preexisting condition for poverty, discrimination, and death. Anti-Black racism is a festering sore, a putrid hole in the soul of America that will heal only with our shared commitment to imagining another way, and to walking that path with furious intention.

There is work for our elected leaders to do, but we can't abdicate the responsibilities wholly to them. We are the ones we've been waiting for to write a new American story, to find a way to build fierce love in the world. We don't have to think of ourselves as activists or organizers to do this work. Every day, like flossing and brushing our teeth, like praying or meditating, we can make choices toward justice, fairness, and equality. We must connect across our differences and build strategies for a better tomorrow for the children we are called to love.

We are the ones we've been waiting for to write a new American story, to find a way to build fierce love in the world. We don't have to think of ourselves as activists or organizers to do this work. Every day, like flossing and brushing our teeth, like praying or meditating, we can make choices toward justice, fairness, and equality.

Children Are Watching and Listening

This may be one of the most important strategies we can enact to dismantle racism: We can teach our children because they are watching all of us. What you show your children matters, and how you talk about it informs how they think about it. They are watching and listening to what we invite into our homes via television, to what we stream or see at the movies, and to our opinions about the ethnicities and gender roles we see on those screens. They hear not only the news but also the commentary we offer while watching it. They take their cues about disagreements from the way we talk about our opponents. What do we say about these people? How do we label them? What do we ascribe to ethnic groups or genders? How do we talk about our opponents?

My mother understood this. She took care to explain what was good, right, fair, and just; what was unfair, unjust, cheating, and just plain wrong. This was a woman who prayed every day, on her knees, before she left her bedroom. She also made a ritual of kneeling by the beds of her children, teaching us how to talk to God. Together, we named the people we loved and strangers we would never meet and asked God to bless them. Our grandmothers and the president, our cousins and people in prison, children down the street or children in India—we asked God to bless them all. We asked God to bless our enemies, whoever they might be, because Mom said we should.

As our family grew, and I grew up, Mom taught me and my siblings to save one-tenth of our allowance and give it to the church, to charity, or to other people. She gave us piggy banks for Christmas to make this practice fun. For Halloween we put money in the One Great Hour of Sharing boxes we got at church, so some child across the globe could eat. We donated some of our savings to the Heifer Project to send livestock to African villages for children and their families. Every day, it seemed, she gave us lessons on what it meant to love our neighbors as we loved ourselves. These lessons from Mom—my first pastor and teacher—have shaped my private life and my public theology and ministry for decades. Mom instilled in me a daily spiritual practice grounded in a simple question: What would Love have me do today?

By the time I was five, I had watched my mom at least 1,825 days, and knew to listen when she spoke of the work her Uncle George was doing to register Blacks to vote. He and Mrs. Fannie Lou Hamer walked up and down the dusty roads in Ruleville, Mississippi, registering their neighbors, undeterred by the taunts and threats of some whites, or even by the shots one of them fired at his house. I considered his work heroic, but Mom, interpreting the world for me, said: "Uncle George and Mrs. Hamer—they were ordinary people making everyday choices for justice. That's how we make the world better."

And then on June 21, three weeks after my fifth birthday, three young men, one Black and two Jewish—James Chaney, Andrew Goodman, and Michael "Mickey" Schwerner—set out to do what was, unfortunately, too common a task. As fieldworkers for the Congress of Racial Equality, they were assigned to Meridian, Mississippi, organizing voters during Freedom Summer. They were asked to investigate the bombing of one of the Freedom School sites, the Mt. Zion Methodist Church, near Philadelphia, Mississippi. But their investigation drew the community's rage; the three men were arrested that afternoon and held for several hours on alleged traffic violations. They were released later that day and followed by local deputies, who were themselves part of the Klan or who tipped off Klansmen about the release. That was the last time the three young men were seen alive. Their badly decomposed bodies were discovered under a nearby earthen dam six weeks later. It seemed that Goodman and Schwerner had died from single gunshot wounds to the chest, and that Chaney, the Black man, had been savagely beaten to death. Just as I remember Mom's reaction to Lisa's calling me the N-word, I remember her sorrow, her bitter grief, when news of these murders emerged. She wept, she swore, she prayed.

Children absorb the love we show them, and the hate we show others. And what about the targets of that hate? What have their eyes seen over time, over generations? What have their hearts taken in? Every day that an Indigenous child watched her family suffer at the hands of white Europeans, and every day that she was forced to let go of her language and culture, she was learning about her place in society and her lack of value in the eyes of her conquerors. Every day that a Black child perspired in the cotton fields, his hands cut and chafed; every day that he watched his parents weep from exhaustion, hunger, and abuse; every day that he cowered behind a shelter and watched whips flay the flesh of his relatives, he was learning about the evils of racism, and how it could strip him of his dignity and God-given worth.

And every little girl or boy of European descent who was nursed by a Black mammy—each one of them taught that she was fit to feed them but unfit to be in charge of her own destiny—was being baptized into a racial hierarchy. Every child who happened upon a postcard showing a group of white people smiling alongside a tree from which a Black body hung like "strange fruit"—a postcard once displayed and readily available—was witnessing the horror that humans are capable of and even encouraged to do to one another.

Those children have ingested racial prejudice deep into their psyches; they either let it become code for their lives or they rejected the very premise of white superiority and did something about it. Who will you choose to teach your children to be? What will you teach them about what is loving, just, and fair? Our job is to help them choose fierce love.

In the Name of Religion

I'm always a little startled by the Church's denial about how long Christianity and white nationalism have danced together. After all, a toxic cocktail of white Protestant nationalism, moral racial purity, and virulent xenophobia is what gave rise to the Ku Klux Klan. And even though the Christian faith is built on the life of a poor, brown, Jewish baby from Palestine who was at once homeless and a refugee; this so-called Christian nation, "under God, with liberty and justice for all" enacts immigration, housing, and voting policies that contradict the biblical mandate to love. And despite the moral teachings of Jesus to love your neighbor as yourself—even when that neighbor is a stranger—Sunday morning worship in most places is still quite segregated.

How did we get here? The answer lies in the very founding philosophies of our democracy. In 1493, a papal bull—an official decree—played a central role in the Spanish conquest of the New World. It stated that any land not inhabited by Christians was available to be **discovered**, claimed, and exploited by Christian rulers. This "Doctrine of Discovery," as it was called, became the basis of all European claims in the Americas as well as the foundation for the United States' western expansion.

For much of Christian history, it's also been the case that many saw no conflict between keeping the faith and keeping or trading enslaved human beings. Indeed, there was once such a thing as a "Slave Bible," a version of the King James that contained only "select parts" of the scripture. Its publishers deliberately removed portions of the text, such as the Exodus story, that could inspire hope for liberation, and instead emphasized texts justifying the system of slavery so vital to the British Empire. One theologian, Harvard-educated James Henley Thornwell, regularly defended slavery and promoted white supremacy from his pulpit in Columbia, South Carolina. In a famous sermon, delivered in 1861, Thornwell preached, "As long as that [African] race, in its comparative degradation, co-exists side by side with the white, bondage is its normal condition." As Rev. Dr. Martin Luther King Jr. would lament a century later in a handwritten letter from the jail in Birmingham, Alabama, the Church has often been silent and sometimes vocally sanctioned the status quo.

Before the fire that destroyed the Middle Collegiate Church in 2020, portraits of all the senior ministers who have served in the church's four hundred-year history hung on the walls in our art deco social gathering space. Among them was a portrait of a minister who owned Africans. But then there was also one of me, with my dreadlocks shining and with my signature red lip. Since its founding in 1628, I am the first African American, the first person of color, and the first woman hired—in 2004—as a senior minister in charge in the Collegiate Church. It clearly took a long time for this particular stained-glass ceiling to be broken! I'm proud to be in this role, in a job I love, but I'm not proud of some parts of our history. I'm embarrassed and ashamed to confess that my ecclesiastical ancestors not only engaged in the slave trade but also "bought" **Mannahatta**—the hilly land—from the Lenape people who lived and flourished on it. But as I look at the Collegiate Church today, thank goodness we've made some reparations.

Now it is in the Collegiate Church's mission to dismantle injustice. We are led by two African American women, one Black Puerto Rican woman, and two white men, one of them our first openly gay senior minister. Among us, we offer food pantries and fight for a living wage; we work to rebuild Puerto Rico and fight for justice at the Mexican border; we work on interfaith relationships between Muslims, Christians, and Jews; we work for LGBTQIA+ justice and gender equality.

At Middle Church, we offer national conferences to train ethical leaders in the tools and tactics necessary to create a racially just society. The killing of

Trayvon Martin galvanized our work and clarified our calling. The picture of our congregation wearing hoodies in worship, in solidarity with Trayvon, went viral around the globe. From toddlers to seniors, we took photos holding signs that read, "I'm not dangerous." Every year, we offer a Martin Luther King Jr. teach-in on the anniversary of his birth, covering topics from the cradle-to-prison pipeline to the implications of the Thirteenth Amendment to how to raise anti-racist children. In 2020, some six thousand people attended anti-racist trainings designed and hosted by our community.

Perhaps the most important reparation Middle Church has done is to put **anti-racist** at the center of our identity, our vision, and our mission. Our movement includes people from many faiths, and also agnostics and atheists who resonate with the ubiquitous call to **love neighbor, posse, and the world** as you love yourself. This ethic of "Love. Period." is our compass that points to healing our souls and the world. In the spirit of ubuntu, we know that we are inextricably connected, and the choices we make every day impact our families, our posse, and our world. Love is our God; the teachings of Rabbi Jesus and the prophets—including modern ones like Ella Baker and Martin Luther King Jr.—are what ground our work. People across generations come to Middle Church, whose diversity looks like the subway, whose worship feels like good therapy.

Fierce Imagination

Once when I was speaking in Washington, DC, at an event to raise awareness for the ways poverty demeans and victimizes people, I looked out from the podium to see a family I recognized from our congregation. There, pushing a stroller with twin boys, was Amanda; her husband, Graham, was carrying their baby girl. It was raining, raw, cold, but there they were, ready to march. She of Kentucky accent and New York take-no-bullshit; he of strong and sensitive support. I've since hired Amanda as part of the church staff. She writes a blog—**Raising Imagination**—about how to raise children who care about the world. She and Graham practice what they preach. The kids go to the polls with Mom and Dad, they talk about race, gender, and sexuality with Mom and Dad. They're aware of the brokenness around them and conscious that they are responsible to be light in the world, every day. They know it will take a village to make a better tomorrow. As Amanda puts it, "We white people are never fully absolved from the way whiteness forms and shapes us and our culture, and it's up to us to lead by example."

Curtiss and Christine, a successful and kind middle-class white couple, choose to bring their children to Middle Church because they want them to know how to live in a multiethnic, economically diverse world in which all genders and sexual orientations are celebrated. They want their children to have the gift of living on the borders of different cultures, so they can navigate the complexity of race, class, and ethnicity in this country with love and appreciation for the unique particularity of each human being.

James and Elaine Wu also cultivate an everyday practice of revolutionary love with their three children. After church on Sundays, the Wu family makes sandwiches for the hungry and takes them to the park. In so doing, the kids have learned about hospitality and kindness. James and Elaine also have a ritual of inviting new clergy to their house for a dinner of steak or oxtails, a practice that drives home the idea of hospitality and kindness each time.

Fabienne and Brent have two biracial children who have turned out to be musical, artistic, and sensitive. As a family, they all also engage in volunteer activities and in activism; they were among the congregants who wore hoodies in solidarity with Trayvon Martin. As these children have grown older, they attend church less often, but Fabienne and Brent don't force the issue. Mom and Dad have continued to lead their children by example: They started a nonprofit to support the rebuilding of Haiti, and they've been part of our Voters Reform

Group, writing postcards and making calls during elections. From where they shop to the news they consume to the books they buy their kids—these parents support each other and make everyday choices to raise love warriors.

I encounter all kinds of people outside of my church community who are also intentional about how they live their lives so they can love the world. Artists who create salons or videos to put love in the world. Botanists who use their hands to grow food and flowers for others to enjoy. Musicians who score music, who sing about revolution, who cultivate peace in their personal relationships. Dance companies that use their art to mentor all kinds of children into living life as lovers of the world. Poets, actors, and producers. This world is full of people who have faith in love and who live that love out loud as justice. I'm so inspired by each example.

What would it mean for you to encourage fierce imagination in your children, to teach them to make everyday choices to love the world? Consider the many books that depict a multicultural, multi-ethnic, just society that celebrates gender, sexuality, and different faiths. Which will you put on your children's shelves so that they will learn about the great diversity in the human family?

Turn the television on with intention. Expose your children to history, music, dance, and art from the many cultures that make up our nation and our world. Travel to museums (you can do this digitally if you need to) and talk with your children about what is there. If you are curious, those who are watching you, studying you, will be curious, too. Do you have a faith community or go to a Y? Is it culturally diverse? If not, you can make a different choice, so your children will have the opportunity to learn in that kind of space. Does your family still celebrate Columbus Day? If you do, do you complexify that celebration with conversations about Indigenous people who lived here before the land was "discovered"? How can you teach children to question traditions that hurt or harm others?

———

The children in your life are
watching you, and learning.
They're not too young to learn
to be anti-racist and pro–racial
justice. They already notice
shades of skin tone and hair, and
other physical traits. If you don't
talk to them about race
and culture, some other story
will fill the silence.

———

As I absorbed right from wrong from my mother, the children in your life are watching you, and learning. They're not too young to learn to be anti-racist and pro–racial justice. They already notice shades of skin tone and hair, and other physical traits. If you don't talk to them about race and culture, some other story will fill the silence. "Colorblindness" is a fallacy and not a lesson we want to teach. We want to delight in difference, to be awestruck and curious about the differences our children encounter. Those differences represent the great diversity of the human species. Normalize racial and cultural differences by speaking of them. Help children register what they see and make meaning of it. For example, **When you saw that white lady on the news yelling at the Black man, what did you think was going on?** These conversations can develop skills of perception and empathy that lead to a more just society. As the author Jennifer Harvey puts it, "Seeing such identifiable differences as a cause for celebration, rather than a cause for differently valuing one another, is essential for putting us on the path away from division and toward racial reconciliation."

Each of us has the power to change the world around us, to build a more just society, to be the change we seek. This is not just true for parents or people raising, teaching, and mentoring children. Each individual person has a sphere of influence. How we behave with friends and families, the stories shared in social media, conversations in the marketplace, how we vote and where we take a stand—these all testify to the values we have.

The Ubuntu Village

Dr. Ruby Sales—human-rights activist and long-distance runner for justice—is my surrogate mama, mentor, and friend. When Ruby was a little girl and fell down and hurt herself, her mom would ask the obvious question: "Where does it hurt?" But it was not only physical hurt that her mother sought to identify and heal. And it was not only her mother who cared. Rocked in the bosom of what she calls Black Folks Religion, Ruby was nurtured by a village of "spiritual geniuses" who knew how to heal the hurts in their community.

While their children were watching, the parents and grandparents in the village raised the imagination of their children, giving them a spiritual language and vocabulary that made them resilient in the face of a nation that did not see them as fully human or recognize the divine spark in them. Ruby learned in her family, in her community, that she was who she was because they each were who they were. She discovered that she had power over her destiny because her people reminded her that though some folks thought they could have power over Black bodies, they didn't have power over Black hearts and souls. Ruby learned that she could sing, "I love everybody in my heart," and that included all the people, even the ones who hated her. Ruby came to know, and never forgot, that no one could turn her heart toward hatred, that she had agency over her own life through love. The children and the elders in her community were all theologians, all speaking, singing, and rehearsing the power of Love to redeem their souls and the souls of their oppressors.

Working as an organizer in Lowndes County, Alabama, Ruby experienced the prejudice, violence, and brutality of the South firsthand. Her friend, Rev. Jonathan Daniels, was killed when he jumped in front of a shotgun blast intended for Ruby. Despite this racial trauma, Ruby is stubbornly committed to the redemption of the souls of all Americans, including the white ones. She believes the culture of American whiteness impacts all of us, robbing even white people of their particularity. She worries that in a broken culture even white people sometimes give up on one another. Ruby works to fuel fierce imagination, to help us see ourselves as more than our racial/ethnic identity. It's Ruby's life that makes her believe in humankind. She learned in her ubuntu village that through love, justice, and relationships—articulated and lived out even in the heat of hot-mess times—we can redeem the soul of America. When I turn my gaze toward Mama Ruby and watch her be who she is in the world, I imagine this to be true. I watch and learn from this woman, who has every right to hate white people because of what she has experienced but instead calls all of us to fierce love.

Alice Walker wrote: "Helped are those who find the courage to do at least one small thing each day to help the existence of another—plant, animal, river, or human being. They shall be joined by a multitude of the timid." A movement to build a more just society begins with little steps taken by good people every day. Humankind desperately needs a love revolution that leads to equality and equity, to the end of white supremacy once and for all. You have the power to be an agent of change in your everyday living; you can influence your posse to also be the change you seek. And ultimately, together, in community, small steps can lead to morally courageous behavior that loves the world all the way to healing.

———

A movement to build a more just society begins with little steps taken by good people every day. . . . You have the power to be an agent of change in your everyday living; you can influence your posse to also be the change you seek. And ultimately, together,

in community, small steps can
lead to morally courageous
behavior that loves the world all
the way to healing.

———

Just as you've come to understand that you can reduce your carbon footprint by making choices every day about the use of plastic and the consumption of gasoline, you can also make daily choices to be anti-racist. You can confront racist conversations at work and at home; you can decide not to consume racist news and social media. You can spend your money in establishments that have anti-racist hiring practices. You can buy from companies that are owned and run by BIPOC—Black, Indigenous, and people of color. Every single day, you can make choices to advocate for LGBTQIA+ communities, for immigration reform, for the rights of women to earn the same as men for the same work. Fierce love demands daily small steps from each of us in order to love the world into healing. These small steps add up to make a better life for us, and a better world for all of us.

You may not feel like a love warrior, **but you are.** Every single day, you have the chance to be the change, to do the right thing, to say the impactful thing that makes a difference. You have the opportunity to use your finances and passion in service of a good cause. You have the chance to ask someone who looks different than you do, someone of another racial ethnic identity, "Where does it hurt?" Even when you can't speak to them, you can be a conscientious student of the things that hurt folks. You can keep watching mentors and mamas, you can keep learning about racial dynamics. You can seek out the skills, tools, and tactics that help to disrupt racism in our nation. You can be a role model for the children in your life, so they grow up to make everyday choices for equality and fairness. You can live justly and help the next generation do the same thing. Dr. Cornel West reminds us never to forget that justice is what love looks like in public. If you and I are intentional, if we make a choice each day to speak out, to stand up for the Love Revolution that will heal our souls and the world, those choices will change you and change your circumstances. Just **imagine** what we can do, together, if we own our power every single day to live justly, to choose fairness and equality.

Chapter Eight

Find Joy Purposefully.
It Is the Water of Life.

When you do things from your soul, you
feel a river moving in you, a joy.
—**Rumi**

The world can be a hard place, and our problems
can feel daunting. It's often impossible to laugh or
smile with so much horror in the news. But identifying and amplifying things that give you joy will
sustain you during the times you're weighed down
by life's injustices—those aimed at you or at others.
Joy is fuel for fierce love.

I'm part of a movement of revolutionary lovers—
faith leaders across the nation who connect around
a movement of justice and liberation. Our community is Sikh and Muslim, Jewish and Christian,

Buddhist and Hindu. We are ordained clergy and lay leaders, poets and preachers, teachers and artists, lawyers and lobbyists. We are a multiethnic rainbow of humans who raise babies, care for our elders, cook for our partners, march in the streets, write op-eds and discuss justice issues on radio and television. Some of us are senior fellows at Auburn Seminary. We are a river—moving, pulsing, picking up stories along the way. This community holds me, supports me and my work. It restores my soul as we build a multifaith movement together, moving like a current. We talk, cry, laugh, gather, organize, play, dance, worship, march, and love the world into healing, together. We work hard, we play hard. We enjoy one another.

———

The world can be a hard place,
and our problems can feel
daunting. It's often impossible
to laugh or smile with so much
horror in the news. But identifying
and amplifying things that give
you joy will sustain you during
the times you're weighed down
by life's injustices—those aimed
at you or at others. Joy is fuel for
fierce love.

———

Sometimes it's all of us doing the work, sometimes it's just a few. Sometimes I'm in the river, wading in the water, conjuring goodness, hands outstretched to the universe, praying, crying, preaching or teaching, organizing, protesting. Sometimes I'm not in the river; I'm tagged out. It's not my turn. I'm on the sidelines, coaching, cheering, supporting, doing social media, strategizing. Sometimes getting in the river means getting in a car.

On the day that nine Black worshipers at Emanuel African Methodist Episcopal Church in Charleston, South Carolina, were killed by a white supremacist, hundreds of us in the movement were at a conference in Washington, DC. We were all devastated at this violence and began to organize a response. After conferring with some of our posse, four of us decided to go down to Charleston to see how we could be of service. After talking to people on the ground about where we might be needed, we checked plane and train schedules and realized that driving would be the most expedient. So, four women—Melinda, Holly, Lindsay, and I—rented a car and drove. While we were on the road, others were already at work. Sikh activist and author Valarie Kaur used the platform she created—Groundswell—to collect prayers from the nation to present to the grieving congregation. The petition that she and our team circulated read:

We stand in solidarity with you in the aftermath of this horrific racially-motivated hate crime. Know that you are not alone. We mourn with you. We pray with you. We stand with you.

Why is this important?

On Wednesday night, a gunman opened fire in a historic African American church—at least 9 people were killed, including the pastor. The shooting is the largest attack on a faith community in recent US history.

As people of many faiths and beliefs—Christian, Muslim, Jewish, Sikh, Buddhist, Hindu, Pagan, Humanist, and others—our hands tremble with the horror and grief of this bloodshed in a sacred space.

We must move quickly to show the community of Emanuel African Methodist Episcopal Church our solidarity, and that we are equally horrified by this shooting.

We stand with the Charleston community and reject the hateful actions of this shooter. And we pledge our love and support as the community mourns and begins to heal.

How it will be delivered

After you add your name in solidarity, a box appears that says "Tell others why you signed"—offer your prayer or message there. **We will deliver your prayers in the next 48 hours.**

In just over two days, we collected ten thousand prayers and delivered them to the elderly auntie of one of the slain. The hashtag we used for the campaign—#propheticgrief—trended second only to #FathersDay, which was in fact that same day. No one person did that. The river did that. And though it was a solemn effort, we were energized by one another's company.

Indeed, we "women of the car" connected deeply and joyfully on that trip. We listened to music and sang whenever we needed cell phone breaks as we drove south. We pooled resources to eat barbecue, pay for the rental car, and buy gas. Lindsay's parents hosted us on the way south. We called ahead and asked for fried chicken, which was served with cole slaw and love. We shared beds like little girls and told our stories and giggled until the wee hours of the morning. We squeezed together in the bathrooms, doing morning routines. We ate the best fluffy biscuits and drank coffee and then went on our way.

Back in the car, we continued to organize, making our way to the pain and sorrow of a community. We grieved that such tragedies could happen in our nation. We went to the church fondly called Mother Emanuel, and laid down our flowers, joined protests, and sang with the bereaved.

We were bonding in the sorrow and in the hard work of doing something meaningful, in bearing witness to the horrific tragedy and to the outpouring of love sent to Mother Emanuel from citizens of all stripes. But when we weren't weeping, we were rejoicing in being alive and in being together. Our lives have been busy and full since that fateful trip, but we're still in the river together. We've marched together, spoken at events together, taught classes together. We hold one another's hearts.

When my church burned down, I received such beautiful love notes from the people in the river with me, activists and movement builders all over the globe. I also received love notes from the three women who went to Charleston with me, signed #womeninthecarlove. That care, that support, those memories bring me joy and cheer me when I'm down.

Joy in Your Superpowers

One of the Auburn Senior Fellows is Rev. Dr. Otis Moss III, the senior pastor of Trinity United Church of Christ in Chicago. He's a preacher, a poet, and, as it turns out, an expert in identifying superpowers. Who knew? At one of our gatherings, we shared intimate stories about our failures, and then listened deeply as we interpreted for one another the superpowers we heard in the stories. Those vulnerable moments stay with us, sustaining us, making us resilient, giving us joy. And listening to our stories, Otis saw us and named us. Me? I'm Storm, because apparently I can change the weather. He tells me that I can make it rain or send a rainbow.

All of my friends have superpowers, and we take turns leading the way. We've got pastors, an imam, rabbis, a comedian, bishops, authors, professors, lobbyists, organizers, musicians, filmmakers, attorneys, activists, singers, and now a US senator in Rev. Dr. Raphael Warnock of Georgia. Together we've got humility and humor. We've had huge wins and we have made mistakes huge enough to learn from. We also have goofy, earnest, sincere, bossy, grumpy, and wild covered. These are my people. I can be all of myself—and all of my selves—in the company of these stunning leaders.

You and yours have superpowers, too. Some of them are obvious and shiny; they can be seen from far away. Some are quiet strengths, best observed up close and personal. At first, some might seem more like weaknesses, but power grows right in the place where you are troubled, worried, doubtful. Vulnerability—which some may think of as weak—is one of the greatest superpowers of all. And in your everyday living, discovering your powers can be a source of joy, like taking that first step, or catching that first ball, or comforting your child for the first time. It's the joy of attending your first march or sending that huge batch of postcards to voters. "Can do" brings joy.

You may not think of yourself as an activist, but the river moving for love and justice has many tributaries. A better playground for the school. Arranging for police officers to play basketball with the neighborhood kids. Sending backpacks to schoolchildren in Puerto Rico. Black Lives Matter is a tributary. DACA is one; immigration reform is one. The campaign to end poverty is one. Environmental justice is one. The river pulses, pounds, and moves against Muslim bans, against gun violence, against children in cages, against anti-Semitism and xenophobia.

I think of all who are activating the love revolution—my friends and yours—as drops that adhere to one another, that join together and move, like a river, like a waterfall. These drops become a mighty stream of love and justice powerful enough to wear away the jagged stone of broken systems. They are persistent enough to transform the parched places where injustice chokes the life out of the vulnerable into an oasis of peace.

The drops in the river adhere but also remain distinct, doing what they are each called to do to resist injustice. Some write books, poetry, and articles. Others organize, march, or train leaders. Some teach, sing, write, and play music, or produce conferences and gatherings. All the while making pancakes for children, watching movies with partners, taking soup to sick neighbors, showing patience with teens, and making everyday choices about how to spend money and time building a revolution of love. When my friends and I gather to grow our joy, we dance furiously and reward ourselves with cashews and chocolate.

What's good about this river is that, although it keeps moving, there is room for you when you get back in it. Just as you are, though the river has moved on, **it hasn't moved on from you.** Your people are still in there. Some of them are clinging to the edges, whispering hope, praying encouragement, coaching for better outcomes. Some are in the shallow spots along the bank. Others have waded in deep; they've got the skills for this deep-water moment. No matter what, your people—the other water drops—are in there. They make room for you and for some new love revolutionaries to join in. This river is a national family of lovers, a worldwide web of fierce lovers committed to healing the world. Our resistance is fierce. Our resilience essential. Faith in Love activates us. Joy sustains us, sustains you!

(In)Describable Joy

Can you feel what I mean by **joy**? Joy is a feeling of freedom, of bounce-back, of contentment, of wonder. Joy is a reservoir of goodness that makes you rock back and forth and hug yourself. It makes you smile for no reason, or your smile might prompt it. Joy makes you tilt your head back in a full-throated laugh. Joy comes around the way, on the way, in the interstitial places between now and not yet, tired and rested, broken and healing, worried and hopeful. Sometimes joy is an eruption, a surprise. Sometimes it's just peace way deep down in your belly. It makes your face shine with gladness and contentment. Mother Teresa said joy is strength.

Once a boyfriend at seminary mansplained to me that happiness comes from the outside, but that joy is a spiritual gift that comes from the inside. Maybe, but I believe strongly that joy is not reserved for folks who are spiritual. And joy lasts longer than happiness, I think. Happiness might be the way I feel after eating the perfect milk-chocolate-covered almond, but that feeling is gone with the swallow. Joy persists; it comes from knowing I am loved by a man who will hunt with me while on vacation to find the perfect chocolate-covered almonds, just because I love them. Comparing joy and happiness, Archbishop Tutu thinks joy is the far greater thing.

I find sunrise a deeply moving and joyful experience. I love to wake up early, while it's still dark, and make a game of getting out of bed and our room without disturbing John. I take my laptop to my favorite chair near the large windows in the family room. I stretch my legs out on the ottoman, tuck one of the creamy white couch throws around me, and ease my way into writing. I look out across the sky as it lightens, checking for that first rosy color to come up behind the trees that encircle our yard. A bank of clouds turns orange, the sky shows more periwinkle, and the sun appears low in the sky. Soon it will be such a bright light, I'll have to shift in my chair to avert my eyes. This quiet anticipation of the too-bright light and its aching beauty is deep joy for me. Alone in my chair in the stillness, the only sounds I hear are the birds coming to feast at our feeder, my fingers tapping on the keyboard, and the soft, creaking sounds of the house yawning and stretching awake.

I tap into joy when I'm dancing with John to my favorite Earth, Wind & Fire CD or his Eagles. I feel it when I sit down to a perfect summer meal: a juicy steak cooked on the grill, fresh New Jersey corn, heirloom tomatoes, and laughter. Joy washes over me when I'm standing on my feet and clapping as the gospel choir at Middle Church sings, "Ain't gonna let nobody turn me 'round." Sometimes, joy creeps up on me, as when I'm sitting on the floor in front of John in his favorite chair. We're listening to some easy jazz or watching **West Wing** reruns—each of which we have memorized—and catching up on the days we've each had during the commercials. He reaches down automatically and gently touches my hair. Those quiet moments with John are precious and too rare in a life that is too busy far too often. My inner introvert finds joy in John's quiet soul. He slows my heartbeat and I breathe more deeply when we are close.

When Joel and Gabby come to visit, and their children go down for their naps, we often engage in an uproarious pre-dinner prep and cocktail hour. This is time for catching up while we chop and cut, for teasing and talk while enjoying a glass of wine. We do politics and mutual coaching; we learn from our children—our joyful, sweet daughter-in-law and our smart, wickedly funny son—what we should be watching, reading, or listening to. Joel is white, like his dad, and Gabby is Jamaican American. The four of us ponder the dynamics in our interracial family. We imagine a reality show, **Black (and White) Like Us**, and how much people would laugh with us at our antics. Our banter can be scandalous. **Will we be seasoning that chicken the "white" way tonight or the "black" way?!** In a time when the racial dynamics in our nation range from toxic to violent, I delight in our little multiethnic, multicultural family, our ability to laugh at our cultural differences, and the joy and playfulness we find in our friendship. There is not a time when our children have visited that we don't feel buoyed, a little more ready to face what the world will throw our way next.

Lessons from Little Ones

Children seem to tap into joy effortlessly, even when engaging in the mundane. We would do well to follow their lead.

Octavius—our grandbaby boy—is the most joyful child, whose deep-throated laughter is contagious. Dancing to music, humming along, bouncing his butt in what the young people call a twerk, he enjoys himself, and cracks himself up. Toddling, he laughs when he falls down, and when he gets up again. His hiccups surprise him and make him delirious. Octavius loves to beat joyfully on his mom's djembe, on the family room table, and on pots and pans; this is a little drummer boy in the making. While watching big sis Ophelia do anything, he is mesmerized with joy. Banging his sippy cup on the table between bites of food, consumed with unbridled pleasure, is one of his favorite games.

Ophelia can sometimes take or leave food, but when she loves it—spicy Mexican food, chicken noodle soup, pasta, and salmon—she delights in it. If a new taste passes the test, she squeals, "I **like** it!!" Ophelia moves through life making up songs, sometimes to melodies she's creating, sometimes to familiar tunes. She sings, "Mommy I love you, Daddy I love you, Pop Pop I love you. Yes I do; I do," to the tune of "Skip to My Lou." After dinner, hands and face cleaned, Ophelia finds introverted joy watching television. She needs this private time as much as she needs the dance parties her parents throw on Friday nights, or dance recitals she herself organizes when we come to visit. She's got choreography for the full scores of **Moana** and **Frozen**. I delight in the invitations to "Dance with me, Nana." When I collapse on the floor, Ophelia climbs up, stands on my belly, and demands, "Get up, Nana!" I could get really fit if I lived with this little girl. To watch her dance with abandon is to witness joy in motion.

Ophelia loves taking baths in Nana's bathroom. She carefully picks which toys will join her in the bath. When the tub is full enough, I turn on the jets and this girl splashes joyfully and howls in delight. She also loves wrestling with Pop Pop, her special friend. "Come with me, Pop Pop," is her invitation to play. Ophelia climbs on John as if he is Mount Everest and has taught Octavius to do the same. She's also taught him how to play peek-a-boo and to play chase through the house. They both howl with laughter and surprise in these moments.

As is true for the adults in their lives, these children—all children—have ups and downs. Octavius never likes being left out of the action and gets cranky if you turn your attention away. He is very upset if we are slow getting food in front of him. Ophelia has **never** enjoyed having her diaper changed, and it takes the work of a well-coordinated village to give her medicine, amid her loud protests. But children—most children—are resilient. They grow their resilience muscles if they're encouraged to be honest about their feelings of frustration or sorrow or anger. They're never too young to be coached on how to be truthful about what's inside them. "Okay," Joel will say to Ophelia. "We can see that you're upset. Would you like to take a breath? Do you need some privacy?" Ophelia is learning at the tender age of three that just being alive causes ups and downs in our emotions, and her parents make space for them all. She's learning that her authentic self can hurt, heal, and bounce back with resilience to joy.

Resilience and joy don't come from being false; they emerge from looking squarely at the truth of our circumstances, feeling what's inside authentically, and then turning a grateful heart toward the good, the bad, and the ugly as part of living a life. This is an important lesson for children and for adults as we face the world.

———

Resilience and joy don't come
from being false; they emerge from
looking squarely at the truth of
our circumstances, feeling what's
inside authentically, and then
turning a grateful heart toward the
good, the bad, and the ugly as
part of living a life.

———

Gabby and Joel are so good about capturing their children's joy in photos and videos, and John and I delight in receiving proof of it.

One of my favorite videos was taken by Gabby and Joel as the babies watched our Rev. Dr. Martin Luther King Jr. holiday worship on the big-screen television in their family room. Archival footage of our multicultural gospel choir was playing. Ophelia mounted her pink-and-purple stool and began to dance. She lost her balance, fell gently to the ground, laughed, and climbed up again. Octavius was watching her intently, delighting in her. He "sang" in his deep baby-boy voice and wiggled to keep the beat. In the end, when I raise my hands to give a blessing to the congregation, Ophelia stretches her arms wide to touch my hands on the screen. John and I have watched that video dozens of times and laughed so hard it hurt each time. In it, Gabby is singing, Joel is laughing; the family is bathed in joy.

Our grandchildren have been imbued with their parents' humor, creativity, and love of life. In short, joy is contagious. And it goes both ways. As is true for so many modern parents, the combination of work and raising children often leaves Joel and Gabby exhausted. Their children's laughter is a tonic. When Octavius is bouncing, singing, and twerking; when Ophelia is dancing, singing, and twirling, Gabby and Joel—and the child inside each of them—giggle through their fatigue.

When you were a child, you had unfettered access to wonder, curiosity, joy, and resilience. You splashed in puddles, you danced and laughed loudly. You need these superpowers now to do the work of justice and equity, to live a life in this complicated world. Watch. Listen to the children around you. See the one reading to herself, the one making up songs? See the one building Legos, and the one painting messily? See the wrestling, tickling, laughing, teasing? See the silliness and the happiness that comes from simply breathing? That joy is yours; it's inside you, waiting to be unleashed.

When you close your eyes and imagine the things you do from your soul that feel like a river of joy, what do you see? Take a deep breath on that vision, exhale, and repeat. Even as you exhale, hold that thought; let it give you pleasure. Let it grow your joy muscle. Claiming joy amplifies it.

We all have the capacity for childlike joy. Simple things like kissing a loved one, stroking the fur on one's pet, even forcing a smile can cause the release of dopamine and serotonin, two types of neurotransmitters in the brain that are heavily associated with joy. The smell of lilacs in the park, the sensation of a grape bursting in your mouth, the feeling of a hot bath—these sensory prompts deliver a burst of joy necessary to sustain the difficult work of healing the world and the everyday work of being human on the planet.

Times of wonder, a make-you-dance track, and sunshine can ignite the feeling of joy, so essential to life itself.

Joy in Middle Church

If you're lucky, if you look for it, you might find joy in your work. I am energized by the joy I've found in my job. Middle Church is my joy jam!

I first came to Middle Church to study the congregation and its pastor, Rev. Gordon Dragt, as part of my doctoral dissertation. I was curious about why churches are still so segregated on Sunday mornings. I wondered what kinds of experiences clergy needed under their belts in order to grow multiethnic, multicultural congregations and what kinds of skills were required. More than that, was there something in their stories, something in their psychological makeup that made it easier for some leaders than others? And if so, could it be taught and duplicated? I had a hypothesis that there was indeed something psychological at work, that something in the development of personality facilitated living on the border, something that enabled certain leaders to hold circumstances in a both/ and kind of way. Studying Gordon, having deep conversations with all kinds of people at Middle Church—I fell in love with them, and they fell in love with me. I started work there on Christmas Eve 2003.

How can I describe this place? Our amazing multi-everything congregants represent every ethnicity, all genders, all sexualities, every generation. The music is sometimes like Broadway, sometimes like a classical concert, sometimes like a gospel revival, and often all of it in one morning. In some churches, passing the peace means turn to your neighbor and shake hands. At Middle Church, this can take twenty minutes—everyone wants to touch **everyone**. Pre-COVID, hugs, slaps on the back, the occasional handshake, and New York–style air-kisses meant holy chaos. Even in the digital spaces we found ourselves during the pandemic, the eye-to-eye connections on Zoom were deep and meaningful substitutions for physical connection.

Our worship is music, art, puppets, dancing down the aisles and on the pews. It's children preaching, it's tap dance, it's candlelight and silk streamers and rainbow balloons. It's theater, its poetry, it's an artist painting on a giant canvas while worship is happening. There's joy from our teens rapping; joy from our toddlers clapping, dancing, and swapping toys during worship. Joy is the only way to describe what we find together. It's what gives us the stuff to go out and resist injustice. It's what makes us resilient in the face of ongoing discrimination based on race, class, gender, and sexuality. It's what helps us survive.

But it's not just a joyful worship experience, it's joyful resistance of injustice. On any given Sunday at

Middle Collegiate Church, there is a wild wrestling with the deep troubles of the world. Theologies of personal piety that lead to salvation do not suffice. There is no sense that praying hard enough will earn a reward from God or allow us to parachute out of this world and into the next. God's love is what motivates us to love one another. Our multifaith community (which includes agnostics and atheists) takes seriously the prayer said every Sunday: "God's will be done on earth as it is in heaven." For us, faith means partnering with God, whom we call by many names—including **Love**—to make heaven on earth. That means healing the world of brokenness; that means working hard to dismantle systems of oppression. That means accepting this: **If there is such a thing as salvation, then none of us are saved until all of us are saved**. Saved from poverty, saved from racism and xenophobia. Saved from gender inequality and discrimination based on whom we love.

In the spirit of ubuntu, we know we can heal ourselves only by healing the world around us. Therefore, though we are having a joyful throwdown, heartbreaking realities are addressed in worship. We take on the foundations of our democracy and oppressive systems woven into its fabric. Our joy-fueled activism points love at the prison-industrial complex and at helping formerly incarcerated people make a just and successful reentry into life at home. We turn joy-fueled resistance onto reuniting children with their families and to eradicating unjust treatment at the border.

At Middle Church we talk about the hard stuff, preach and teach on the hard stuff. Weep, shout, shake our fists about the hard stuff. Protest and march about the hard stuff. And, in the same space, we sing, laugh, hug it out, play, and dance. Alice Walker wrote, "Hard times require furious dancing. Each of us is the proof." Amen! From Alicia Keys's urban beats to Bach, from gospel to jazz— our music is sung in the key of life. Nothing is too secular to be sacred; all of it is holy. Our children serve the elements when we celebrate Communion or Eucharist; they need no fancy degrees to be seen as ministers, either. We believe joy will keep us agile, open, and energized. It fills us back up when we are depleted and restores our souls. Our holy texts tell us weeping will last for a night, but joy will come in the morning.

Healing Joy

Joy has been the fuel for resistance for centuries and across ethnicities, but the Black joy found in the African American experience is of particular importance to me. Those resilient Africans who survived the terrible, dehumanizing Middle Passage found a way to gather, to sing, to dance, to pray, to drum out their sorrows. Merging the Indigenous spiritualities and cosmologies they brought with them from home—in which their ancestors played a prominent role—with whatever resonated from the religion taught to them by their masters, Africans cultivated resilience and joy in the brush harbors, the secret meeting places deep in the woods—covered by tree branches and quilts—where they snuck away to worship freely.

Using spirituals like "Steal Away to Jesus" as code, the leaders of this "invisible church" called enslaved Africans out of their cabins and into the night. Someone kept watch for slave patrols while others began to sing. Deep in the woods, those gathered were free to shout and dance and shout some more, as they did back home: dancing in a circle, uniting with their ancestors and deities—and whichever Christian "gods" were resonating in their difficult circumstances—in worship. Grounded in joy and hope, their worship helped many steal away to the road to freedom, or to be free in their minds.

Alongside the Black Lives Matter movement, or maybe I should say inside it, there is a movement afoot about Black Joy. Joy, creativity, laughter, affection, and eroticism are essential to well-being and health for all people; and Black people are talking about it as we talk about how our lives matter. Black folks have cultivated joy in order to survive the onslaught of violence and anti-Black racism that has been our experience in this nation. Black Joy is resilience. As one song suggests, the world didn't give it to us, and the world can't take it away.

Pride and Joy

In my life as a pastor and public theologian, in all of my speaking and writing, I teach this: Every human life is precious, each human is divine. I celebrate the unique particularities and gifts of all peoples and have worked with my staff and lay leaders to cultivate a community that represents the great diversity of the world. As such, at Middle Church, along with Black Joy, there is Puerto Rican and Dominican and Chinese and Japanese and Dutch and German joy in the space, and other racial/ethnic joy as well. There is also queer joy in the space. Pride Month is like Christmas. We sing pop songs, like "I'm Coming Out," as hymns. Dressed in our "Love. Period." T-shirts, we dance to Beyoncé as we boisterously greet one another.

One of my favorite days each year is Pride Sunday. Worship is a party, for sure, with both choirs singing. But when it's over, we leave in groups to head to the subway. We make our way uptown to the place our float waits in the Pride Parade lineup. Here we gather, in our shirts, sun protection, and sunglasses, some of us pushing babies in strollers. While we wait for the march to start, we sing and dance to the music playing from our float. At my granddaughter Ophelia's second march, she grabbed hands with some other children and they danced, joyfully.

When we set off on the parade route, when the

float turns down Fifth Avenue and meets up with the other marchers, carrying our banners, it's as if more lights turn on. The energy is off the charts; the **thump bump thump** of the bass in the music, the laughter, the costumes are all so wonderful. It's a day to lose weight; we dance all the way down the avenue until we turn off at Christopher Street in the West Village. And while we're dancing and singing, we're hugging the often-surprised folks who line the streets. It's clear in their reaction that they've never seen a church like this! And they are confused, delighted, and surprised to see our "Love. Period." banner flying behind our multicultural choir. **Love is love is love**, we are saying, singing, demonstrating. One year, our church received an award for best float! When we take it to the streets, embracing our joy, it's reflected back to us. Joy amplifies joy.

Joy and Generosity

Embracing joy also breeds generosity. Edna Benitez, a deacon at Middle Church, is a living example of the connection between joy and generosity. Her efforts at rebuilding Puerto Rico are both heroic and contagious. She has raised money, inviting her friends and family to partner with her in the work, and has launched an effort to put roofs on soggy buildings. Edna lost a family member to the crumbling (or nonexistent) infrastructure in Puerto Rico. Still, she fights on. From making sofrito with the Lower Eastside Girls Club to chairing the benevolence committee of the oldest church in North America and directing funds toward a deaf community in the mountains, Edna maintains a commitment to Puerto Rico that testifies to what we can each do, if we put resources where our hearts are.

Giving our time, our energy, and our money to support the causes and people and movements we believe in puts power in the system, puts our own skin in the game, and puts joy in our step. Edna dreamed a world of healing in Puerto Rico, and you can, too. You can become a committed stakeholder in the society you want to create. The outcomes matter when you are invested, when the success of the mission is your success, too. You know the joy you feel when you find just the right gift for your beloved, and they are surprised to get it? How they delight in knowing that you know them enough to pick out that perfect item for them? That's the joy I get from giving to my church and other charities that matter to me. The Dalai Lama says generosity is a natural outward expression of inner compassion and kindness. For me, generosity extroverts my inner joy.

Friends, I believe the bold path to making our lives and the world better is fundamentally lit by the radical, fierce love that all the major religions preach. Though we are outraged by injustice, we don't get there with just our outrage. We need to get there with our joy, which—according to my friend Father Richard Rohr—is both a decision and a surrender. It's a decision to look around and recognize and value what is good, what is lovely, what is inspirational—and let that delight us. It's surrendering to the fact that there is not much we can control in life, but our reactions are within our control. Recognizing joy and embracing it—these are our decisions to make.

Every Day, Joy

What gives you joy? To notice it, to write it down, to deeply feel the moment is to cultivate it. To cultivate and claim joy is itself an act of resistance. It's a worthwhile daily spiritual practice. Joy will keep your heart pumping with love, your mind cooking with ideas, and your body jazzed with resilience for this journey called life. Joy fuels the resistance and resilience required to make a better life and a better world.

———

Joy will keep your heart pumping with love, your mind cooking with ideas, and your body jazzed with resilience for this journey called life. Joy fuels the resistance and resilience required to make a better life and a better world.

———

What if, while eating, you gave in to the delight of what's on your plate? What if you tuned in to and were mindful of the musical sound of your children's laughter? What if you cultivated joy with your partner by making a daily ritual of a joy respite together? What if a ten-minute foot-rub or tickle-fest, a fifteen-minute daily dance party, or a twenty-minute tea break became part of the routine for you and your household?

What if you spent time writing in your journal, noticing the things for which you have gratitude? You might look in the mirror every morning and take note that you are alive, breathing, strong, and badass. You might breathe deeply and meditate on all the goodness around you. You might start each day saluting the sun, either on your yoga mat or outside in a jacket with your thermos of coffee. You might spend a few moments on the way to bed on your phone, not on social media, but in your photo file. Go to the photos or videos that make you laugh out loud and watch them nightly. Pray thanksgiving, if prayer is your thing, or make a gratitude ritual every night on the way to sleep. Let your mind drift from complaining to sustaining your soul with fierce love and joy.

On any given day, your joy might be quiet and peace-filled, tucked way down in your belly. Your joy might be extroverted and raucous, making you dance, sing, and shout. Do **you** with your joy, **be** you with your joy, feel it your own way. Every day, like brushing your teeth, focus on it, find it, be fueled by it. It's inside you, waiting to resource you. To build your resistance and resilience. It will support you, whether in your movement-building or when making sandwiches for your children. It will help you stand up for the other and stand in line for an inoculation. Joy powers kindness; joy begets joy.

Joy is an essential need for the thriving of the human spirit. Without it, we are diminished and too often left with the festering of our wounds, resentments, and fears. Joy is that feeling of well-being, pleasure, and happiness that accompanies us as we move through life. It alters the way we see the world, its people, and ourselves. Joy tints our perspective with optimism and the confidence that we will go through the hard things, and though we might be bruised or battered, we'll come out on the other side. Joy is the wellspring of resistance, the water of life. Now, close your eyes, take a deep breath, and smile from the inside out. There, there it is. Can you feel it? That's joy!

Chapter Nine

Believe Assiduously.
Have Faith in Love.

My religion is very simple.
My religion is kindness.
—Dalai Lama

The definition of religion, according to several dictionaries is **the belief in or acknowledgment of some superhuman power or powers (esp. a god or gods) which is typically manifested in obedience, reverence, and worship.** The root word for religion is the Latin **religare**, from **re-ligare** or **re-ligo**, which means to re-bind, or to bind again.

In its truest sense, religion should reconnect human beings—bind them again—to the creation, to one another, to the Divine, to Love. Rituals, song, prayer, preaching, reflection, dancing, meditation—all of these religious practices are intended to bind us together in love and restrain us from harming one another. Religion should reconnect us to the ground of our being, to the source of our existence. Religion should help us listen to the calling of our better angels. It should improve our ubuntu sensibility and help us see how much we need one another to survive and thrive. Religion should help us see how our biases about color, gender, sexuality, and class cause deep hurt to both body and soul.

Unfortunately, religion is too often weaponized. Wars are waged in the name of religion. People are enslaved and terrorized in the name of religion. Wealth has been amassed on the backs of the poor in the name of religion. I'm a Christian pastor, and these are things **my** tribe has done, all in the name of Jesus. Jews were exterminated, in the name of a poor, brown, **Jewish** baby who was at one time homeless and at another a refugee.

If humankind is to thrive, we need to let go of any religion that wounds and kills. Some of what we believe about God is **actually** about us; at times we create God in our own image. In other words, some of us imagine **God** as punitive, angry, and vengeful because these are aspects of ourselves that make us feel powerful and protected, rather than vulnerable. But we need to exercise a spiritual imagination free of fear and shed the constraints of unhealthy religion. Hate-filled religion needs an exorcism!

In the interest of exorcising hate, I find myself preaching and teaching folks to see through the eyes of Love, to believe with all their heart in Love. I invite them to worship Love, to pray to Love, to be part of Love. I find myself counseling people that **becoming love itself** will heal them, and when I feel playful I offer this blessing at the end of worship, to laughter: "Go out in the world and make love, everywhere." It's not that I've lost my religion, it's that I've found another one. My new religion is Love. Fierce Love. Period. This is all that matters.

Outside Church

In fact, if it weren't for the amazing, artistic, creative worship at Middle Church, I'm not sure I'd worship in a church at all. When we're on vacation, John and I worship in nature, near water. It might be on a beach with surf bubbling and waves cascading, tickling the sand and then running away again. Whether on a cold, rocky shore, with the surf pounding away at boulders, or a wide sloping beach with soft pink sand littered with seashells, or a narrow strip of a beach with sharp little shards of lava—being near water is our thing. For us, it is like heaven.

Often, we find sanctuary in our backyard, near our pond. We love to sit on a big, flat rock and dangle our feet in the water. From there we see all the colors of our yard. So many greens to describe on our trees: some bluish, others with hints of yellow; lilac bushes and hydrangeas; purple lilies around the pond. The colors of this sanctuary outdo stained-glass windows any day! We sit there listening to the sound of the two waterfalls our friend George, who built the pond, created with rocks and electric pumps; watching birds bathing and deer taking a drink; being mesmerized by our fish playing. They fascinate us, hypnotize us. Even on a hot, muggy New Jersey day, my soul is refreshed when I stick my feet in the cool water. If I move my feet just the right way, our fish come and nibble my toes, bringing with them a riot of gold, orange, red, and white with black-and-purple markings.

Two years ago, during a long, cold, and snowy winter, a weasel slithered through our pond and ate all of our fish. They had been named by a niece, by neighborhood children. They had given birth to little fish, growing our original five koi to forty adults and babies of various sizes and colors. And they were all gone. We shed a tear for the fish, even as we understood the weasel itself took them, no doubt, to feed her own babies. We missed our colorful pets. But we waited for two years, hoping to discourage our pond as a food source, then bought six more koi. They're just as beautiful as the ones we lost.

One bright morning thereafter, I found myself drinking coffee and dangling my feet in the pond.

I marveled at all I could see. Bees hovering close by, a hummingbird kissing the lilies as they opened. Mosquitoes and gnats landing on blades of grass and dive-bombing my eyes and ears. I shaded my eyes to peer into the water and I was startled to discover that there were new, teeny tiny babies in the pond. Someone did **not** use their birth control! There were so many little fish—orange, yellow, and red fish everywhere. Looking more closely, I noticed literally **scores** of little black fish that I had missed. Black fish—some black with even blacker markings, some spotted black—swimming, eating, playing with the other little fish, hiding more easily than the more colorful fish, near the deep green moss.

How did these black babies emerge from a pond full of white, orange, and gold creatures? Curious, I turned my attention to Google and discovered that among the varieties of koi, two major black color patterns exist—the Bekko have small black dots, and Utsuri have large patches of black and their coloring is genetically determined. These little black fish can and did come from the more colorful breeders.

While reading, my mind drifted to my own coloring, and to John's, and to what it's like to hold hands with him on the beach, at the pond, or in church, and see the contrast. How the levels of melanin in my deep brown skin and in his fair skin are also determined by genetics. How this coloring set our lives in motion in a world ruled by racial hierarchy. How racism is real, but race is not. How genetically, there is only one race, and that's human. How the concept of race was largely made up by Johann Blumenbach, an eighteenth-century German anatomist who declared that the white people from the Caucasus mountains were the superior race; and Samuel Morton, a nineteenth-century scientist from Philadelphia who collected and measured skulls to prove Blumenbach right. How the human genome project has proven that **all** humans, no matter our coloring, originate from Africa. How anti-Blackness is so ironic, so tragic, given this fact. Frowning, I forced myself back to the fish in my pond, and the differences in their coloring, and to the fact that, though different in coloring, they are all koi.

As Far as the Eye Can't See

John and I bought our house thinking we might retire here. It sits in a small development, outside Clinton, New Jersey, up on a hill on land that the Lenape first inhabited and from which iron ore was mined for a century. When we asked our friend George to build the pond, he and his team dug a huge hole in our yard, removing countless boulders. Using a tractor, they created a path through the wilderness to put the boulders deep into the woods, laid plastic on the path, and covered it with small stones. This is the path that deer, foxes, and bears use to get to the pond to drink, to taste our raspberries. From down this path, we often hear the sounds of mewing fawns and coyotes.

At night, the path is dark and scary. Even the fullest moon lights only so much, before the darkness swallows the light. I'm embarrassed to tell you that this city girl is always a little afraid outside by myself at night. On the porch, in the hot tub, under the moonlit sky, I squint, and peer down the path, imagining the bear that has been on our porch, eaten our bird food, and slapped on the sliding glass doors. A bear once removed the hot tub cover and drank our water. It's not a stretch to imagine a bear looking back at me, or maybe it's the coyote we hear at night. To calm myself, I close my eyes and imagine the doe and her twin fawns instead. Anything else is terrifying.

What we can't see can be frightening. I think this is how it is with God. We can't see God, so we peer into the mystery and try to imagine what's peering back. Sometimes we imagine a terrible, awful thing, the stuff of our worst nightmares, a vengeful God who will claw away at us or our enemies, like a bear or coyote, and rip away flesh. Or a God who will hear our misery and turn away and leave us all alone. We might imagine a God who will set upon the world a scourge like COVID-19 or HIV/

AIDS, or create a hell on earth like the California wildfires, because we've misbehaved.

We might, however, peer into the mystery, into the darkness, and be comforted by the image of a loving, nurturing, sheltering God. A creating God in whose womb we abide; a warm, soothing, way-making darkness, a merciful darkness in which we are nurtured and rocked to sleep. A rich darkness, like soil, with good stuff for us, the stuff we need to grow. Maybe we see safety in the darkness, and it feels like home.

Sometimes we imagine the mystery as beauty. Maybe God is a lovely, curly-haired child who could belong to any of us; or maybe we see God in nature, in the beauty of fish in a pond and the miracle of procreation; in the artful sunset over an ocean; in evergreen trees tipped in snow. We imagine God as a good shepherd or a shelter in a time of storm. We choose images and metaphors because we actually don't know what lies on the path. Of course, not knowing is perfectly okay, as is rejecting the notion of a deity altogether. We fill the mysterious hole in our imagination with what we need to survive. Since I can't truly see what belongs in that space, I've chosen most recently to put LOVE in that space.

Believing Is Seeing

All of us who pray to God see our way to doing so, making a leap of faith. What's also true is that even those of us who make a living writing, thinking, and talking about God are all making **assumptions** about God shaped by the testimony of others, texts we've studied, fears, experiences, yearnings, and hopes. How we talk about God is informed by snippets of memory, song lyrics, and how we were parented. When our idealized parents loved us so much, they felt like God to us, or like the God we long for. We're impatient to know what the mystery is, and, not knowing, we try to find ways to connect. Maybe if we devour it, conquer it, we will have its characteristics. Maybe if we make sacrifices to it, pray to it, dance for it, we will be blessed. And so we chant about it, sing about it, dream about the mystery. My own recurring dream always seems to go something like this:

> I'm a child, about seven or eight, and I'm on a mountain. I'm traveling around and around it, going higher at every turn, passing through the four seasons. Everywhere I look, there is life. Buds are bursting green into bright summer light, while warm breezes caress my face. Leaves are turning golden and crimson, then falling and baring their nakedness. There's snow everywhere, making soft ground cover, decorating treetops like frosting on cake. New life is pushing up through cold earth at springtime, creeks and rivers filling with melting snow.

I walk through the four seasons over and over again on my way to the top. In the end, at winter, there's a giant lion with a huge face—not scary, kind of friendly. His shaggy white mane is covered in snow. Each time I come to the end of my climb, I see the giant lion, the compelling green eyes, intensely focused on mine. Each time, he speaks words I can't understand no matter how hard I try. I lean in to listen, I squint, trying to read his lips, but I can't see well enough to do so. I know somehow that if I were able to hear more clearly, to see what he was saying, to understand him, I would know how to heal the world.

My dream, in fact, my whole life, leaves me feeling this: If there is a God, there is something about God in what we see as we climb our way through life. Something in the changing of seasons, in the falling leaves, the melting snow, and the sun-kissed faces of the people we love. The rotting vegetation, the browning grass, the dying fish, and the full belly of the weasel. The way the fox will eat the weasel, the way the turkey buzzards will eat the carcass of the fox. The way the warm follows the cold, and the way life insists on itself.

If there is a God, there is something about God in the way humans see their way to slog through life, with love. The way my friend Meghan puts her little girls to bed with the sitter and goes to work in a hospital operating room—especially worrisome during the pandemic. The way she dons her protective gear, saves the lives she can, then goes back home. Taking a hot shower, thinking about death and life, she sleeps some, then wakes up to do it all again the next day. The way social workers and teachers and parents and bus drivers and police officers and activists and artists and clergy and farmworkers and grocery store clerks all do essential work, all part of the circle of healing, the circle of pain, the circle of death, the circle of life. God is in that.

There is something about God in the way the universe shows off to us, something in what we see as we gaze upon stars and moon and sun; something in the red cardinal and the blue jay, in the mewing deer, the stealthy fox, the harmless-but-huge bear. God is in the way we strain to listen, to hear what is being expressed that helps our eyes and our hearts see further, better. The cries of babies, immigrants in cages, and the cries for justice in the streets. The voices of scientists and health-care workers about the reality of climate change and the dangers of a pandemic. There is something about listening to one another in truth-filled conversations at the dinner table or the boardroom table or in a Zoom meeting that helps us to better see the souls of our neighbors. There is even something of God in the horror we see on our screens. Indeed, it was the sight of George Floyd being crushed to death that sent thousands to the streets and into anti-racism trainings in the summer of 2020. They wanted to understand and change the way that skin color and the value attributed to it led to one man kneeling on another's neck until he was dead. We need to see, for what we can see we can face, and as James Baldwin reminded us, what we face we can change.

A few years ago, I was in Israel with some Christian clergy, studying ethics with a rabbi named Donniel Hartman. Exploring the Hebrew texts concerning caring for neighbors, strangers, and enemies, Rabbi Hartman said:

"A life of faith isn't just about walking with God but how one walks with humanity. If you find the donkey of your enemy, return it. If it falls down, help it up. You must do this even if there is no one around to see you. You must do this with anything that your fellow human has lost and you find; you mustn't remain indifferent. **The core feature of a moral life is to see.** Choosing not to see is immoral. The goal of religion is to improve our willingness and our ability to see." A spiritual life is supposed to help us see better. The aim of Love and any God worth worshiping is improved sight.

The Hazards of Not Seeing

Sometimes I don't see so well. Once, before I had two cataracts removed, John and I were at the grocery store. I picked up a bottle of that creamy, vanilla-flavored goodness that turns coffee into dessert. I squinted to read the label and then showed it to my husband to confirm my hope that the calories per serving were just three. John burst my bubble; turns out there are thirty-five.

Even with the cataracts removed, sometimes I still can't see. I can't see how the fleeting look of impatience on my face can hurt my husband's feelings. I can't see how I am just like my mother in so many amazing ways, and also in the annoying way I ask questions rapid-fire. **Are you okay, John? Do you need water? Can I get you some lunch? Are you okay? What are you thinking about now?** I want to connect with him so badly; when he is feeling introverted, I insist on interrupting his peace with my need to help. I can't see how that chases him into the next room, creating more distance.

Sometimes, I can neither see nor hear how much I talk. As we worked at home together in the summer of 2020, John would often set up his work in a different room because, he explained, he couldn't work when I was talking. I promised not to use the phone in a shared space, but he pointed out that I don't need to be on the phone to talk, that I talk to the air—I talk to anyone and everyone, no matter if they are listening. Until he pointed this out, I didn't really see (or hear) myself clearly.

What **else** can't I see, what else don't I know?!? I simply sometimes can't see my stuff. When I jump into helping mode before John finishes his sentence, it shuts him down, and I am suddenly on his last nerve.

In my work, sometimes I can't see that being direct and clear is essential to being supportive and encouraging; that when I overvalue being nice, it weakens my intention and confuses my message. Sometimes I can't see that the only person I can control is me; that in painful interactions, I can change me and my response, but not the other person. Sometimes I can't see that I am engaging with the addictive behavior of a friend or a congregant, nor can I see how I medicate myself with work.

We all have problems seeing. We sometimes can't see that until we love ourselves, we are not fully able to love others, that forgiving ourselves gives us spiritual and ethical power with which to be healers in the world. Because the world rewards "nice," we sometimes can't see how powerfully liberating it is to speak the truth in love. We sometimes can't see the importance of downsizing the emotional burdens we carry so we can live justly and fairly every day. We can be blind to the fact that in order to be healers of the broken spaces in ourselves and in the world, we need radical truth-telling and moral courage. The eyes of our hearts can't fully comprehend how essential joy is to fortify our resilience and resistance, and how opening our hands and hearts generously can change the world around us. We sometimes are unable to see that we become our best selves in relationship. With this truth as our guide, we can see each other into thriving and wholeness.

There are costs to our inability to see, and we know this. Indigenous people, women, queer people, Black people—they were not seen by our nation's founders, are seldom seen now with appropriate value, and our nation still pays the price. As I've said before, race still seems to be the **different difference.** Black wealth doesn't compare to white wealth. Black health doesn't, either. And Black men, women, and children are arrested and incarcerated at rates disproportionate to our percentage of the population. It sometimes seems as though our cherished Lady Justice—designed to be blindfolded—is actually blind to her biases.

If we are willing to look closely at ourselves and our stories, we can see just how much each of us has been blinded with bias. When we don't see, we miss the truth: that we are one species, one human race, sharing genetic material and a common origin in Africa. We are bound together; our liberation and thriving are tied together. When we can't see one another, when we don't see the connection, we are less human. Of course, as we seek to see one another, what appears to be one thing may indeed be something else altogether. What looks like anger might be sadness. What looks like bitterness might be grief. What masquerades as bravado might be insecurity. What looks like retreat might be the bravest move, a time-out to come back strong and win with love.

We are bound together; our liberation and thriving are tied together. When we can't see one another, when we don't see the connection, we are less human.

Belief in You, Me, and Love

While I've retreated from some of what the church has taught—women are inferior, queer people are sinners, white people are predestined to rule the world, non-Christians are doomed to hell—I've doubled down on my belief in love. It's my North Star. There's a text in the Christian scriptures that reads: "God is love. Those who abide in love abide in God and God abides in them" (1 John 4:16). It reminds us that when God's people wandered through the wilderness, they built a **mishkan**—a dwelling or tabernacle—in which God could reside with them on their journeys. It was light and portable and could move as the nomadic people moved. God, the scripture says, resides everywhere love is. When you love, God lives in you. **That makes you a love shack, baby!**

I'm not trying to convince you about God; I'm trying to get you to believe assiduously, to paraphrase a scripture from my tradition, that **love is the only way, the only truth, and the only life**. No one religion has all the truth, but love is the truest truth I know. My life has been transformed by revolutionary, fierce love. I've been saved from depression and anger by love given to me with force and grace. Angels have watched over me with love. I've been midwifed and given birth to myself by love. I'm deeply connected to my dad because of love. I've seen love drive millions into the streets to declare, "Love Wins," and I'm a believer.

I also believe in you and me. We've got all the things we need to make this world just, fair, grace-filled, peaceful, and loving. Once, when preaching a sermon about how much time Jesus spent with those considered to be outsiders, I said: "Jesus welcomed the tax collectors and the sinners; he made room for the bullies, the thieves, the lepers, and those considered sinners. We need more hymns about that crazy kind of welcoming love." On his way home from worship, my friend Tituss Burgess started writing an album for Middle Church. One of the songs, "We're the Ones," has this verse:

> **I sat back waiting, anticipating at some point change would begin**
> **But then it hit me, I was what was missing;**
> **My weight was dead, that's why we couldn't get ahead.**
> **So no more delays, it all ends today.**

It don't have to be so heavy if we'll all carry our
   weight
You and I are the ones we've been waiting for.
You and I thought this was somebody else's war,
You and I are the ones, the ones we've been wait-
   ing for.

We're the ones to welcome all of those who are
outside to come in from the cold to the warm fellowship of love. We can do it, and we must. There
is simply too much at stake for the status quo to
continue. We must see our way to it, together.
I know we can because I see evidence that good
people all over the planet are making it happen.

We must, like the interfaith group of leaders who
recently saw their Muslim sister demonized during a series of protests against police brutality and
risked their own positions of power and prestige to
say: "Enough. She is one of us; get off her back." We
must take a stand, like two artists, Genesis Be and
Aunjanue Ellis, and risk time, arrest, and resources
to stand against the Confederate symbolism in the
Mississippi state flag. They persisted, and the flag
was taken down! We must as humanity, no matter
our gender, march against sexual predators and for
the voices of women. We must take ourselves, as a
group of leaders did recently, to the Texas-Mexico
border to bear witness to the sites of terror and
demand the release of parents and children because
they are our children, too. When we stand for the

value of Black lives, that must include the vulnerable lives of fierce Black trans women; their lives matter, too. We must see something, say something, and do something.

One cold January day in 2015, some of the leaders in my congregation took a chartered bus uptown to Harlem, where we picked up friends from Union and Auburn Theological Seminaries. It was 5:00 a.m. and still dark outside when we drove across the George Washington Bridge, trying to sleep a little more. Those of us who were wide awake whispered anxiously about what would happen when we got to the Longworth House Office Building in Washington, DC. Many of the US representatives have office space in Longworth; it seemed like a good place for some civil disobedience against lethal policing. Two Black men from my congregation, one gay and one straight, confessed their fear. "We're going to protest violent policing; what if the policing gets violent today?"

The plan was to stage a 4½-minute "die-in"—a minute for every hour Michael Brown lay in the street in Ferguson, Missouri—in the Longworth cafeteria during lunchtime. Our bus dropped us off at a Methodist church, where we freshened up, ate breakfast, and loaded up on coffee. The leaders of the action gave us instructions and signs to carry.

The plan was to enter the cafeteria singing—itself an infraction—then spread out in the front of the room where there was the most space. On cue, we'd chant, "Black Lives Matter," and then lie down on the floor. Experts told us that most of the time, the police were patient until the third warning—then there would be arrests. We agreed we would stay down for as long as we could bear it, until the final warning, then we would all get up and leave. We organized ourselves outside in the cold, and marched as a love army—multiethnic, interfaith, intergenerational, secular, and spiritual leaders—from the church to the Longhorn Building.

It was one of the first congressional sessions of the new year, and the cafeteria was busy. In what some of us call an ethical spectacle, we sang, chanted, and then lay down on the ground, close together, holding signs on our chest that read "I can't breathe," "Hands up, don't shoot," "Black Lives Matter," and the names of some of the dead: Rekia Boyd, Eric Garner, Yvette Smith, Michael Brown. We settled into our positions on the floor, making adjustments, squeezing closer together. I lifted my head for just a moment, so I could see our fifty bodies from my vantage point on the edge of the crowd. Some had locked arms; in the closeness of the space, legs touched arms, arms touched torsos, heads were connected like one. We were all one body; not just those of us there but all of the fallen, the lynched, the casualties to a racist culture. And we were all the living, breathing legacy of John Lewis, Ruby Sales, Stokely Carmichael, Martin Luther King Jr., and so many more, charged with holding America to her promise of democracy.

We chanted, we sang, we chanted some more. The crowded cafeteria hushed and grew noisy again, responding to our clamor, some staring, some recording or taking pictures on their phones. One woman standing near me said, "Wow, I never thought I'd see something like this here."

And then the Capitol Police came.

You are here unlawfully, and we are giving you a chance to leave. This is your first warning.

It felt as though time slowed down. I heard the sound of foot traffic, the sound of rustling coats and restlessness.

You are here unlawfully, and we will arrest you. This is your second warning.

I saw shiny black boots out of the corner of my eye and realized my heart was beating fast. I'd seen on film what boots can do.

More boots walking near, more rustling, whispers. Should we get up? Not yet. Someone squeezed my hand.

This is your final warning.

Then the leaders were moving among us. **Get up now, get up quickly now, and walk to the door,** they said. And: **Let's sing.** I led,

Ain't gonna let nobody turn me round.
Gonna keep on walkin', keep on talkin', marchin'
   up to Freedom Land.

We were one body leaving the building, one body making our way back to the bus. I saw more clearly than ever that protest isn't just about what we do, **it's about what people see because of what we do. It's what gets exposed about the system, about us.** See how we lay down together. See the ages and faces and colors and genders. See the children on the bus, on the bridge, in the streets. See how venomous is the response hatred has to love. See the women and men walking to work, skipping the bus. See the millions on the mall, in the street. See how we are one body pulsing, breathing for the ones who no longer breathe. See how love wins time and time again. Can you see we are a movement, a river in motion, until freedom comes? Look in the mirror; see that person? You are in the river, too!

Seeing, Believing, Loving Assiduously

Rabbi Hartman and Congressman Lewis were right: An ethical and moral life is about letting go of indifference and **learning how to see.** It's about waking up to love ourselves, love our posse, and love our world. When we love fiercely, we have the power to change our circumstances and to build a more just society. Imagine this fierce love as our shared spiritual practice. Rather than creating rules and regulations that erect boundaries between tribes and clans, we might practice religion with its true meaning in mind: binding us to one another, enabling us to see our connection, that we are kin. Our faith practices could simply enable us to see our shared humanity, our inextricable connection; this is ubuntu. As Desmond Tutu said: "Ubuntu speaks particularly about the fact that you can't exist as a human being in isolation. It speaks about our interconnectedness. You can't be human all by yourself."

When the Zulu people greet each other, they say, **Sawubona**, which actually translates not to **I see you** but to **WE see you**. Who is "we"? We are me, my ancestors, and the divinities around me. One response, remember, is **Sikhona—I am here; I exist.** Another response is **Yebo, sawubona—I see you seeing me.** Being seen and seeing the other becomes a contract, a covenant. This is ubuntu: We are human only in relation to one another; we are bound in a bundle of life, woven together in a garment of destiny. Whatever affects one of us affects all of us. Injustice, poverty, bigotry—when one of us is wounded, we all are hurt. On the other hand, surviving and thriving with resilience, hope, and joy are also to be shared in the village that is our globe. In the spirit of ubuntu, I'm called to interrogate my life: How will what I freely do impact your freedom? I can make an assiduous commitment to our shared humanity. Why? Because you are my people, and I am yours.

All of the people we see are our people. Our accomplishments and our failings are all tied together. The Republicans, the Democrats, and the Independents; those funding campaigns, those running for election. The ones in cages and the ones living in gated communities. The activists on the street and the law enforcement folks. Students and teachers facing each other on Zoom—we are all neighbors who might lose something and need it returned to us. We all have a mother or a grandfather or an uncle or a child who, laboring under a heavy load, might fall down. We need our neighborhood to take time to help them stand up.

———

All of the people we see are our people. Our accomplishments and our failings are all tied together. The Republicans, the Democrats and the Independents; those funding campaigns, those running for election. The ones in cages and the ones living in gated communities. The activists on the street and the law enforcement folks. Students and teachers facing each other on Zoom—we are all neighbors who might lose

something and need it returned
to us. We all have a mother or a
grandfather or an uncle or a child
who, laboring under a heavy load,
might fall down. We need our
neighborhood to take time to help
them stand up.

———

In the summer of 2020, when the government discontinued extra funds in unemployment checks, when some legislators complained that $400 was too much to give to struggling families—that it would disincentivize their working—my colleague Rev. Dr. Damaris Whittaker began a Cancel Rent program at her church, making grants to congregants so they could stay in their homes. Following her lead, Middle Church passed a budget in which almost 10 percent of it was designated as grants to alleviate poverty, to pay utilities, to put food on tables, to cancel rent and help with mortgage payments. This is what it means to love fiercely, to live ubuntu. We must look at our neighbor fully illuminated by the light of compassion and ask ourselves: What have they lost here, and can I help them find it? Can I return dignity or worth? Can I return compassion or solidarity? Can I return civility to the public discourse and conversations? Can I return kindness? And shall I acknowledge the things that I have lost along the way? Can they be returned to me?

I am a witness to how the people around the globe have claimed me and Middle Church as their own, wanting to return something lost to us. When a fire caused by a neighbor destroyed our sanctuary before Christmas in 2020, thousands of people responded. They sent love notes in e-mail, and on Twitter, Facebook, and Instagram. They sent donations— from as far away as New Zealand, and from around the corner in the East Village. Synagogues, temples, churches, and mosques offered space for us to meet. Tituss Burgess, Shanta Thake, and Charles Randolph-Wright gathered artists in our March to Rise campaign and at Juneteenth to sing, to offer support, to raise money. One January morning, I opened the five hundred messages I had been saving, and read them aloud, to myself, for myself, and wept at the truth of what I preach. Love is seeing. Middle Church and I had been seen by a global community that refused to remain indifferent to our plight.

In order to live a moral life, a good life, an ubuntu life, we must commit to a life of love that means **seeing all the things**. See your neighbor suffering and do something about it. See a stranger laboring under a heavy load and help out. See lies spoken and shared in social media and call foul. See a friend soaring and say, "I see you, beautiful creature!" and build their self-love tank. Love doesn't pretend, love keeps it real. Even when it's difficult and makes people uncomfortable, speaking the truth is the only thing that will set us all free. I want you to see that fierce love boldly confronts systems and situations with moral courage, inviting more humanity from ourselves and from the other. We must even confront our families and friends, when we sit with them to break bread, and they make racist, xenophobic, or homophobic comments about "them." Though we are fearful, we must find the courage to say, "When you speak that way/behave that way, I feel concerned [hurt, angry, disappointed, sad]," and open up a conversation.

Fierce love means seeing the hard things. There was once a white man who worked for me, who persisted in not seeing me. If there was any way for him to avoid my authority, my leadership, he would. He'd go around me, set up conversations without me, exclude me from e-mail chains in which my voice should have been essential. He couldn't deal with my Blackness and my femaleness. I spoke to him one-on-one about this several times before I finally called him into a meeting with a group of leaders. I spoke with as much energy as I could, my voice strong and strident, and told him his behavior was unacceptable. Now, I had said this before, but this time I added that he made me feel unsafe—a truth I could hardly access myself—and the air shifted. This younger-than-I-am white man—one of the white liberals who consider themselves "woke," as opposed to being truly awake—was hurt to think

I felt unsafe. Those were the words that broke open the dynamic, those were the words that **helped him to see me.** Did I change him? Not likely. Did I change the behavior? Some. What I did, by speaking the truth out loud, was open the eyes of that man, as well as those of my other colleagues. Saying what I observed helped them to see things about our system that we could all address, together. Then we were able to get into some important conversations about gender and race.

Love does **not** turn a blind eye to injustice. When maskless masses gather during a global pandemic, that's unjust. When essential workers don't make hazard pay, that's unjust. When school systems barely check on air-conditioning ducts before reopening schools, the school systems and the government need to take notice. Their lack of attention to the children is unjust. We can choose to see how vital it is to keep our children and their teachers alive and healthy; we can see, and we can find our way to different solutions. The community must see and demand this together. We must believe in the power of seeing. And when we see something, let me say it again, we must say something and do something.

Having My Say

Our calling is to fulfill the dream of a loving and just society. I want to convince and convert you.

We are people with such goodness inside, so much love inside to give. I write to encourage you, to enlist your heart in a movement of love and justice that needs your particular voice and viewpoint. You are the only one standing where you stand, seeing what you see, positioned where you are positioned. You are right there for a reason, to have, as my dear friend Ruby Sales says, "hindsight, insight, and foresight." I want us to remove the cataracts from our eyes and learn to see, with our eyes wide open, how best to be healers and transformers. I want us to really see, **to fully awaken** to, the hot-mess times we are in and to the **incredible** power we have to love ourselves into wellness. We are the ones, folks; we are the midwives to help the world give birth to its better self. To learn to walk with whichever higher power speaks to us, we absolutely must walk with one another into tomorrow with full sight. I invite you to believe assiduously in how lovable we each are, and in the love between us and among us because, actually, **believing is seeing.**

Believing is seeing our connection; we are one. This is the kind of fierce love to which we are called. This kind of love is not a feeling or sentiment; it's radical, transformative action that takes risks to seek the common good. It sees our neighbor better than they see themselves. It makes sacrifices, it creates a way out of no way. It's the Black folk religion I grew up with—for **all** of the people. It's the fiercest love of all.

This fierce love is not for the faint, the indolent, or the idle! We can't just **feel** love, we must give love, we must do love, we must be love ourselves. Our calling is to see something, and, seeing it, to call it out and do everything we know is good and just and vital to heal our souls and the world.

Writing this book has been the stuff of my dreams. I wrote it to enlist you in a fierce love army. I want you to help me help our children. I want my grandchildren and my nieces and nephews to live in this world and be seen, known, and loved, not feared. I want to leave them a safe and brave world in which they can play, walk, or jog in their neighborhood; drive; sleep in their beds; and protest without danger to their Black bodies. I want your children to grow up in a world where they can love whom they love, be who they are destined to be, practice any faith or no faith, and honor their calling to care for their global neighbors. I want our progeny to understand ubuntu, to find love in themselves, to grow it for their ever-widening posse, and to build a love movement in the world, for all of us.

I want to convert you, to convince you, to proselytize you. I want you to believe with me in our shared capacity to make a better life and a better world, together. I hope you'll believe assiduously in love, in the fiercest love of all.

I want to convert you, to convince you, to proselytize you. I want you to believe with me in our shared capacity to make a better life and a better world, together. I hope you'll believe assiduously in love, in the fiercest love of all.

Acknowledgments

This book exists because Todd Shuster at Aevitas Creative Management midwifed the idea with me. Todd, what a joy to gestate **Fierce Love** with you! Thank you for mentoring and encouraging me with such patience and faith until we found just the right way to put love in the world. I'm so grateful to Marnie Cochran and the Harmony/Penguin Random House team, who believed in **Fierce Love**; who shepherded and shaped this book with me. Marnie, your kind edits and cheerleading were simply pitch-perfect; I loved working with you. Thank you! Thank you, Christina, Valarie, Paul, and Kaliswa, for reading drafts.

There have been so many people in my life who created the village—the ubuntu village—that taught me fierce love. My siblings—Roderick,

Rodney, Ronald, Wanda, and Richard—were my first friends. I'm so grateful for shared mischief, growing pains, tears, and laughter that make us a posse. Speaking of posse, thank you, cousins on both sides of the family, for memories; and thank you, Aunt Verl, for looking out for me.

I've created family all my life, in Rochester, California, Princeton, Trenton, and New York. I've picked up sisters, brothers, and aunties who've loved me over Chardonnay and coffee, on walks and on retreats. The Senior Fellows at Auburn Seminary help me better see my superpowers and show me theirs. "Storm" thanks you, and so do I, for your love and support, for the ways we heal the world together; and thank you, dear (twin) Katharine, for dreaming us up. Special thanks to my accountability buddies—Macky, Kate, Michael, Patti, Susan, Claudia, Lyn, Tituss, Charles, Felicia, and all the girlfriends who love the world and me fiercely. Thank you, Rosie, Bobbie, Tony, Janel, Garry, Melanie, Morgan, Jordan, Eric, Riz, and the Middle Church young adults (all y'all, so many, so beloved), for loving me along my growing-up and letting my inner child play with you.

I learned how to do justice and love fiercely in the context of my congregations—Imani and Middle Collegiate Church. Though there are not enough words to say for all of what you've etched on my soul, I'll say thank you for loving me and letting me love you back. Thank you, Middle Church family, staff, board, and chairs, for your **incredible** partnership over these years.

My "children"—Gabby and Joel; my grandchildren—Ophelia and Octavius; my nieces—Rio and Jourdan; and my nephews—Rod Jr. and Ron Jr.: You are my present and my future, my hopes and my dreams. Thank you SO much, Dad; you and Mom made me **everything** I am. In the spirit of ubuntu, I am who I am because you are who you are. I love you both fiercely!

Finally, John—it all comes together with you, my love. You are my everything. I'm grateful to see the world, partnered with you.

ABOUT THE AUTHOR

Rev. Jacqueline J. Lewis, PhD, is a public theologian and the senior minister at the progressive, multicultural Middle Collegiate Church in Manhattan. Rev. Dr. Lewis is the first woman and the first Black person to serve as senior minister in the Collegiate Church of New York, which was founded in 1628 and is the oldest continuously operating Protestant church in North America. A graduate of Princeton Seminary and Drew University, she is the creator of the MSNBC online show **Just Faith** and the PBS show **Faith and Justice**, in which she led important conversations about culture and current events. She is also the host of **Love. Period.**, which can be found wherever you listen to podcasts. She curates an annual national conference focused on activism and imagining a more perfect union, Revolutionary Love, and she is the co-producer of the annual star-studded Juneteenth Now—Get Us Free celebration. She has been featured in **The Washington Post**, **The New York Times**, **The Wall Street Journal**, **Ebony**, and **Essence** and has appeared on CBS, CNN, NBC, MSNBC, PBS, and ABC. Rev. Dr. Lewis is a member of the Auburn Senior Fellowship, a group of influential faith leaders who are committed to advancing multifaith movements for justice. Raised mostly in Chicago, she now lives with her husband in Manhattan.